THE JEW TO-DAY

THE JEW TO-DAY

By

SIDNEY DARK

*Author of " The Glory That is France," " The Story
of the Renaissance," " St Thomas of Canterbury,"
" Five Deans," etc., etc.*

The Section on Modern Jewish Philosophers

By

The Rev. A. E. BAKER

LONDON

IVOR NICHOLSON & WATSON LTD.

44 ESSEX STREET

STRAND W.C.2

MCMXXXIII

First Edition . . . November 1933

*Printed in Great Britain by Sherratt & Hughes, at the
St Ann's Press, Manchester*

CONTENTS

To RALPH DAVID BLUMENFELD

MY DEAR RALPH,—*The substance of this book has been in my mind for the last four or five years, based largely on many conversations and arguments I have had with my Jewish friends. The latest outbreak of anti-Semitism in Germany has made the position of the Jew a matter of topical interest, and I have now tried to put into form and order the reflections and conclusions that have resulted from much talk, much reading, and much thought.*

No man, except the unbearable dullard, can claim to approach any human problem in a spirit of strict impartiality and with the certainty that his judgments may not be affected by entirely personal factors. As it has happened, all through my life, I have had contacts—some of them intimate, and continuing for many years—with Jews. Latterly these contacts have been, for one reason or the other, largely increased; and I should suppose that few men outside their community have had greater opportunities for estimating the charms, the deficiencies, the qualities, and the prejudices of English Jews than I have had.

Mr. Hilaire Belloc says that " there is no European so mean in fortune or so base in character as not to feel himself the superior of any Jew, however wealthy, however powerful and (I am afraid I must add) how-

INTRODUCTION

ever good." I am a European, certain comparatively mean in fortune, but I trust not base in character, who has never felt anything so idiotic. I can never remember having disliked a man because he was a Jew, any more than I should say that I had ever liked a man because he was a Jew. Some Jews I have detested, as I have detested many Christians, and other Jews have been, and are, my friends for whose friendship I am immensely grateful. Certainly in the many years during which I worked with you, for a large part of the time as your intimate and trusted lieutenant, I had no sort of feeling, as Hilaire Belloc suggests I ought to have had, that I was in any way your superior. I was not, thank Heaven, such a fool. If I had been, you would certainly roughly and successfully have dispelled the illusion.

Some explanation is perhaps demanded as to why a man who, for nearly ten years, has been insistently concerned with the defence of a definite theological position, should have spent his time in this study of a people, who in nothing have more perplexed the world than in the general rejection of that religion, the greatest factor in modern history, which, with its miraculous and catastrophic inspiration, derives almost entirely from Jewish theology and the Jewish ethic. But the failure of the Jews throughout the centuries to make anything more than the feeblest of responses to the appeal of the Christian Church is one of the reasons why they are of particular interest to the Christian apologist. After the capture of Jerusalem, and the destruction of the earliest of the Christian churches, Christianity became almost entirely non-Jew. Not one of the post-Apostolic fathers was a Jew,

viii

and this was doubtless due to the Jewish reaction against the Hellenistic teaching of St. Paul. The reaction anticipated persecution. The Jewish antipathy to Christian dogma, and particularly to the doctrine of the Trinity, was, without question, immensely increased by persecution—and the persecution, that began in the early centuries of the Christian era, continues to this day. A reasonable sense of shame, therefore, stimulates the desire to attempt, at this particular time and from a non-Jewish point of view, a sympathetic study of a people that has preserved individuality in the face of persistent and unparalleled repression, and that remains, as it has been since the Dispersion, a unique phenomenon in human history.

I have limited myself to the consideration of the Jew and his position in the world, as it exists to-day, and I have only been incidentally concerned with the Jew as he was yesterday and the day before. I have made no attempt to write anything like comprehensive history. My interests have been not with things as they have been but with things as they are, and as they may be. In view of the fact that the Nazi revolution in Germany is the most important and the most menacing event in recent European history, and that Herr Hitler has, as it were, dragged the Jew on to the centre of the world's stage, it does seem to me of some importance that the majority, who are not Jews, should understand the man that the Jew really is, and not as he is painted by his enemies, or as he may seem to himself. It is a matter of little difficulty to show that at least nine-tenths of the charges brought against the Jews by their critics and their enemies are demonstrably untrue, and it is clear to me that a great many of the qualities, that the Jews claim as exclusively theirs, are certainly not exclusively theirs.

The Jew is accused of putting his finger too often and too deeply into the European pie. Hilaire Belloc says: ("The Jew", p. 199):

"The Jew acquired in all the larger communities, and especially in France, Italy, Germany and England, a power out of all proportion to his numbers, and I may add, without, I hope, offending any Jewish reader, out of proportion to his abilities; certainly out of proportion to any right of his to interfere in our affairs."

Such a statement, certainly generally accepted, does not, as I shall show, stand detailed examination. International Jewry, even in the world of finance, is little more than a phrase. The statement in that strange product of American anti-Semitism, "The International Jew", that "Judaism is the most closely organized power on earth" is grotesquely untrue. And, considering the dispersion of the Jews and their cosmopolitan attachments and experience, I regard it as a great misfortune that the Jews of the world do not possess a far greater coherence and a far greater power to act together, not to acquire any sort of domination, not to jerrymander markets, not to set nation against nation, but to be the foundation stone of a genuine and romantic internationalism, which, from the very fact that it would be romantic, would be realistic, for one of the paradoxes of human life is that the two things go together. My contention is that the Jewish influence in the modern world is comparatively small and that it might be infinitely to the advantage of the modern world if it were far greater,

INTRODUCTION

because, owing to his unique position in the history of humanity, the Jew to-day is the only real internationalist.

So, my dear Ralph, in affectionate memory of the years we spent together, and in gratitude for the friendship that has continued unabated since our paths have diverged, I commend this little book to your kindly criticism.

Yours affectionately,

SIDNEY DARK

SAVILE CLUB,
October, 1933

CHAPTER I

BOURGEOIS PAR EXCELLENCE

THEOPHILE GAUTIER divided mankind into the flamboyant and the drab. Youth is nearly always flamboyant, maturity is nearly always drab. And the persistent contest between the flamboyant and the drab is, in part, the contest between youth and maturity. Until medical science added to a man's years, the world remained flamboyant. Indeed, until the Reformation, the flamboyant held, as by right, the centre of the world's stage.

Great men, were they kings or bishops or poets, glittered in their actions as in their raiment. They lived romantically and they died young. Reason had not begun to triumph over instinct, and men had not come to fear high adventure because it had no practical value. Now and again a drab figure, anticipating the *bourgeois* age, appeared on the scene. But Henry II of England was compelled by the dead St. Thomas to an uncomfortable flamboyancy on the stoney streets of Canterbury, and Louis XI of France was forgotten when St. Joan rode in triumph into Orleans. The poor lived hard and their years were few. But they were within the orbit of the flamboyant, else how could the Gothic cathedrals have been built? " The King and

I

the priest," says Mr. Christopher Dawson, "were united to their people by a bond of organic solidarity."

But even with flamboyancy at its zenith, the drab played a part in the world of ever-increasing importance. The Jew, already in Europe for centuries, was outside the social and spiritual order. Schools were shut to him. He could not own land. He was forbidden the armour of the knight and the jerkin of the peasant. He was not permitted to use his skill with the craftsmen of the guilds. In order to live he was compelled to be society's scavanger, to do the work that neither noble nor knight, peasant nor craftsman would do. He became the go-between, the trader, the huckster, the money-lender. He was the first *bourgeois*. For that reason, he became, in Mr. Dawson's phrase, the *bourgeois par excellence*. But he has always been the *bourgeois malgré lui*.

No man possesses a more flamboyant tradition or a more fascinating sequence of flamboyant heroes—Abraham, " very rich in cattle, in silver and in gold "; Joseph, whose life is summarized in his coat of many colours; Moses, who lived romantically from the day he was discovered by Pharoah's daughter in the bulrushes, until his death in the land of Moab (" Moses was an hundred and twenty years old when he died; his eye was not dim nor his natural forces abated "); David, who went out against the Philistine armed with a sling and a stone; Solomon, the Temple Builder. Isaac of York, despised and scorned, was far enough away from the Jews of romance, but it was from the high ethical teaching of his prophets that the Catholic

2

religion and its creation, Western Civilization, had evolved. Perhaps he remembered that it was the Sweet Singer of Israel who had given the Church its songs, and that the moral code that the Christian priest taught his people was a Jewish code. Perhaps, too, he remembered when, buffeted behind the barriers, he watched armoured knights jousting to win their ladies' smiles, that one of the earliest and, as it remains, one of the most exquisite of love songs is the Song of Solomon.

The Jew, indeed, has always remembered. '' The Jew has a racial memory beyond all other men,'' says Mr. Hilaire Belloc. But his memory was all that was left to him. He was fated to be the herald of the drab, when all men loved the flamboyant. He had to hide away his coat of many colours and put on, in its place, the dingy gaberdine.

The drab has conquered. The captains and the kings have departed, taking with them their banners and their trumpets, to be succeeded by the banker, the merchant, and the politician. A *bourgeois* civilization has developed in which the tables of the money-changers are more respected than the altars of the Lord. The world has lost its colour. The revolution began in the sixteenth century, but the triumphs of the drab have been most obvious and universal since the Great War. Now the nations of the East—hitherto patronized as ' backward ' because life remained for them something of an adventure, and the prophet was regarded as of greater account than the placeman—have come into line. The fez has been replaced by the bowler, and the mystery of the harem has been dissipated by free access to the polling-booth.

It might be supposed that the triumph of the drab must be a triumph for the Jew. In truth, it is the cause of his present woes.

The soul of man remains incurably romantic. He may not believe in God; he always believes in fairies. He is bored by the practical, by the expected, by the teachings of experience. "People like licence, and dislike restraint", says T. S. Eliot. "They like surprise. The one thing they do not like is boredom."

Socialists contend that wars to-day are brought about by economic conditions and developments, as they were the result of dynastic jealousies in the centuries before the beginning of Industrialism. That is an illusion. Individuals and nations are affected infinitely more by the romantic and the sentimental than by the practical. National passions may be inflamed by interested persons, eager to add to their bank balances, and it may, therefore, be supposed that the real power that pulls the levers, holds the steering-wheel, and determines destinies is the cold-hearted holder of the money bags. But this century's history sufficiently disposes of the theory.

Suppose—and incidentally it is untrue—that there was complete justification for the assertion of the Peace Treaties that Germany and Germany alone was responsible for the war, then the responsibility would attach not to the bankers nor to the manufacturers and merchants, who, in a few short years, had created a great international trade that threatened the supremacy

4

of Great Britain in every overseas market, but to the dream, the flamboyant dream, enshrined in the phrase *Deutschland über alles*, originally suggesting that for the German Germany always comes first but developing into the dream of a Teutonic domination, so that Asia would be the German washpot, and over western Europe the Kaiser could cast his shoe. Even admitting that this dream was exploited by the militarist, the victory of the flamboyant remains, for the militarist is always affected by a flamboyant tradition, even when he has degenerated into a drab stupidity.

Since the war men without panoply, without prestige, and without vision, have made feverish and entirely unsuccessful efforts to recover lost prosperity, while the drab majority are eagerly praying for the end of war, which means not only that there shall be no more wholesale destruction but that there shall be no more collective romance. I am a pacifist—but I am not young. I only see the ugly and the cruel in war. Part at least of the youth of Great Britain agrees with me. The youth of Germany and Italy certainly do not.

No generation ever deigns to profit by the experience of the generations that have gone before. Mankind persists in the endeavour to test everything by contemporary experience. To-day there is a generation in Europe too young to have been personally seared by the events of the war years, and almost ferociously resentful of the conditions of life that the war has caused. This resentment is naturally most active, and, perhaps, most unintelligent, in the countries that have not only suffered from the general economic chaos, but

B

are bearing the additional moral burden of the stigma of defeat. The Nazi movement in Germany has no clear social or economic policy behind it. It is based on an entirely banal racial theory, but it has attracted the majority of the youth of Germany, because it is essentially a revolt of the flamboyant against the drab and of the romantic against the realist.

Epater le bourgeois. This has always been the slogan of the revolt. The spirit of the Nazis is a vulgarized adaptation of the spirit of the French romanticists. They are inflamed by a similar hatred of the drab as that of Barbey D'Aurévilly, as Edmund Gosse has described him, "with his long, sparse hair flying in the wind, his fierce eyes flashing about him, his hat poised on the side of his head, his famous lace frills turned back over the cuff of his coat, his attitude always erect, defiant and formidable." And it may be said of the Nazis, with the addition of stronger adjectives, as it was said of D'Aurévilly, that they are "fervid, sumptuously, magnificently puerile."

Man has always been, and always will be, swayed by the irrational, or, as the Catholic would say, by the supra-rational. And here I may be permitted the comparative irrelevance, since it is illustrative of my own standpoint, of pointing out that the only institution on earth that is, in its character, essentially flamboyant, while it offers its never failing protection to the drab, is the Catholic Church.

Every political movement for the last hundred and fifty years has either been a revolt of the flamboyant

6

against the drab or of the drab against the flamboyant. The revolution of 1789 was the rising of the drab against the decadent flamboyant, even though, in its early and magnificent stages, the revolution was led by a superb flamboyant in Danton, who was fated, after the manner of his order, to be the victim of the drab Robespierre. The 1830 revolution was essentially a *bourgeois* and a drab revolution. The 1848 revolutions were flamboyant, and drabness may have been said to have established itself with the overthrow of the Paris Commune in 1871.

Successful revolutions have nearly always been religious in their inspiration, even though the religion may have been a false one. For the moment I am not concerned with the philosophic basis of Bolshevism, although this must be considered in any attempt to determine the position of the Jew in the modern world, but there is no question that the success of Bolshevism is due entirely to the fact that it is religious. Mr. Christopher Dawson has said in his book *Enquiries into Religion and Culture*, that Communism " owes its success not to the impersonal evolution of capitalist society, but to the religious fervour of its disciples, their spiritual revolt against the practical materialism of modern culture and their apocalyptic hopes in the realization of a Messianic reign of social justice on earth ". That is to say, Bolshevism, materialistic in its philosophy, is strikingly anti-materialist in its appeal.

Similarly, Fascism in Italy and Hitlerism in Germany are definitely religious movements. Their

7

founders have set the nation upon the altar. They demand from the worshippers of the nation a blind adoration and a complete disregard for the pity, justice, and compassion which are taught by the religion of Christ.

Unless all this is understood, the recent outbreak of anti-Semitism on the Continent must remain a hopeless puzzle. Since the beginning of the industrial revolution, the world has been growing more and more *bourgeois*, and the Jew, I repeat, is the *bourgeois par excellence*. He was the herald of the new order of society, and as that new society has evolved and has become more and more universal, he has remained most typical of its characteristics. It is therefore inevitable that, in every revolt against the tyranny of the *bourgeoisie*, against both its deficiencies and its ideals, the Jew should be the first person to be attacked. By force of circumstances he has become the most notorious champion of the drab, and it is against him that Don Quixote's lance is most eagerly turned.

All this is irrational; but humanity, undirected by the one institution that demonstrates the reasonableness of the unreasonable, and the irrationalism of the rational, must remain befogged, striking wildly, journeying no man knows whither on an uncharted sea.

The sorrows of the Jew and the problem of the Jew, so far as it exists, are only in a very secondary degree affected by his peculiar qualities or by such racial and religious separatism as he has contrived to preserve. Deep-bitten in the majority who are not very intelligent, not very well informed, entirely incapable of foresight and for the most part indifferent to the future, there is a deep resentment of a social order that is colourless and undramatic in its direction and materialist in its judgment. The brown shirts and the black shirts are arrayed against the white shirt and the high collar. The tyranny of a Napoleon will always be accepted with enthusiasm, because Napoleon is picturesque and, as in the case of General Boulanger—an adventurer who was merely picturesque, and was without brains or courage—may on occasion almost succeed in becoming a tyrant. But the tyranny of the market-place is always hated, and it never requires any great effort to stir the people to vicious stone-throwing at the men whom they regard as the agents and ministers of the monarch who, despising the glitter of a golden throne, rules in mysterious secrecy from the gloomy seclusion of a bank-parlour. "We instinctively feel," says Mr. Christopher Dawson, "that there is something honourable about a king, a noble, or a knight, which the banker, the stockbroker, or the democratic politician does not possess."

The Jew, as the *bourgeois par excellence*, is, therefore, particularly hated by the enemies of a *bourgeois* civilization; on the right hand by the adherents of the old order, making a desperate eleventh-hour effort to recover the power that has gone for ever; and, on the left hand, by the multitude, and particularly by undisciplined and inexperienced youth, eager for the recovery of adventure in an age that is timid and apprehensive.

In other words, anti-Semitism is definitely political and social, far more than it is racial. It has, indeed, been political and social for a hundred years.

Mr. Belloc would almost seem to suggest that every good European is an anti-Semite at heart. He says in the book from which I have already quoted (*The Jew*, p. 44):

> When we look round the modern world, say the last twenty years, we discover, in widely separate places, and among very different interests, and inhabiting the most diverse characters, the presence of what is for many a new political feeling: it runs from irritation to exasperation, from grumbling to invective; it is everywhere directed against the Jews.

I do not say that this feeling does not exist. It is evident enough in Germany, in Poland and in Hungary. But I should not have supposed it was world-wide. On the contrary, the indignation aroused by the Nazi anti-Semitism would seem to suggest a widespread appreciation of the Jewish character with the full realization of the Jew's value as a citizen. Speaking in the House of Commons on the German Jews, fleeing from Nazi persecution, Colonel Wedgwood said: "We are now anxious to import foreign capital into this country; how much better it is to import foreign brains and amalgamate them. I do not speak from the obvious humanitarian point of view, but from the point of view of the material advantage of this country. Get these people in." In the complementary debate in the House of Lords, Lord Cecil of Chelwood described the British Jews as "among the most peaceful and orderly citizens of this country"; and Lord Iddesleigh, a Roman Catholic, declared: "My co-religionists and Lord Reading's worked together very successfully and very happily before the recent revolution." In a letter to *The Times*, referring to the boycotting in Germany of Jewish surgeons and physicians, Lord Horder said: "We needs must lose enormously from the sterilization of so fertile a source of knowledge." The words of these four Englishmen do not suggest either irritation or exasperation.

It is idle to attach any great importance to one's own circumscribed experience, but it is a fact for what it is worth that I have never come into personal contact with anti-Semitism in England, or even with pronounced anti-Jewish prejudice. There were a number of Jewish boys at the undistinguished school to which I went. They did not come into prayers in the morning or attend the Scripture lessons, but I have no recollection that they were the target for youthful insolence. As a journalist I worked for years under a brilliant Jew, and I have known a number of Jewish journalists—not, by the way, very many—and I do not believe that they were either helped or hindered by their race. Indeed, English Fleet Street was, in my day, much more apprehensive and resentful of the competition of the Scots and the Irish. Generally I should say that in the world

that I know best, a little more is asked of the Jew
than is asked of other men, and rather less forgiven
him. But that is all. I have put the question, "Have
you ever been humiliated or insulted just because you
were a Jew?" to at least a dozen men of various
positions. Some of them answered that they never
had. Others admitted that, on some few occasions,
they had had uncomfortable experiences. Three of
them, men of different ages, said, "Not since I left
the University." This set me to inquire of both dons
and undergraduates of the present generation. At
neither of the ancient English universities do Jews
particularly favour any one college, but at both they
naturally foregather together, as Roman Catholics
do. Again I am assured that they are received or not
received as individuals. In Oxford and Cambridge,
as in a London Club, what I have written is the rule
—a little more is asked of the Jew than of other men,
and rather less is forgiven him. At London University, as is proved by the remarkable Students' Club
in Russell Square, there is no racial or colour prejudice—the University must surely be the most
democratic institution in the world—and the Jewish
question simply does not arise.

One of my Jewish correspondents has written me:
"All Jews in Christian countries have to overcome
prejudice from their fellows due to the first teachings
on Christianity emphasising the part of the Jews in
the Crucifixion and mentioning little of the part of
the Romans, and never mentioning that the Apostles
were mainly Jews." I have no doubt that this is

largely true, but the prejudice has decreased since the non-Jewish world (as it seems to me, to its infinite loss) has ceased largely to be even nominally Christian. It is unfortunate that the Jew is often vociferous among militant atheists, and that when he retains his ancient faith he sometimes writes very ignorant rubbish of Christ and Christianity as is to be found in such a book as Lewis Browne's *The Story of the Jews*, which, in other respects, has considerable merit. For a Jew to write of Christ in a book, intended for popular English reading: " To some he has become altogether a God, and to others—because so much evil has been done them in his name—he seems very like a fiend ", is, apparently deliberately, to aggravate prejudice. I quote it as an indication that the Jew is, himself, sometimes responsible for the suspicion of which he complains.

But in England the dislike and the suspicion hardly exist. I am assured that in the East-End of London, with its large Jewish population, the little anti-Jewish prejudice, that there was twenty years ago, has disappeared now that immigration from eastern Europe has come to an end, and there is a generation of Jews, educated at the same schools as their fellows, all of them speaking English and a considerable number not speaking Yiddish. I found that " Oh, she's working for the Jews " is a definite expression of contempt. But the Jews are the only people in the crowded districts east of Aldgate ever able to afford a ' help ', and the expression merely conveys the dislike that the factory worker always has for the restrictions of domestic service. Prejudice has been affected by the more common intermarriage and in certain areas, where friendship is most marked, I am told that the non-Jew has become curiously Jewish, eating Jewish food and acquiring certain Jewish characteristics.

Except as the very poor envy those who are less poor and the thriftless dislike the thrifty, Jew and non-Jew live together in amity in the mean streets of England as they live together in the suburbs and the squares. The relations described by Louis Golding in his novel *Magnolia Street* are generally true to the facts.

It may be said that this is the more remarkable since the Englishman is essentially insular, with an instinctive suspicion of the foreign and the strange. But that is not true. It is inconceivable that any people could create a great commercial Empire unless they possessed qualities which made it easy for them "to get on with the foreigner". Such anti-Semitism, therefore, as exists in England, is alien to the national character.

In France, the only other country of which I have any considerable personal knowledge, I have never found any tendency to Jew-baiting except among the readers and admirers of *L'Action Française*. There are comparatively few Jews in France, though they have played as important a part in its cultural life as they have in the cultural life of England, and I do not forget the *affaire Dreyfus*, to which I shall return. In America the Jew, a very newcomer, is undoubtedly regarded with considerable suspicion.

In New York, Jews are not admitted to good clubs, but it must be remembered that there is an enormous number of Jews in New York, and to elect a few Jews would be to risk a club becoming pan-Jew. The "hundred-per-cent-American" movement, the anticipation of Hitlerism, which found its expression in Klu-Klux-Klan was aimed at Jews as well as at Negroes and Roman Catholics. But the movement has apparently died of its own excesses and exaggerations. While the Jew still plays a very small part in the public life of the United States, a Jewish senator is now one of the most important leaders of the Democratic party, and President Roosevelt has appointed another Jew as Ambassador to France.

In this brief survey, my object has been to show that there is no universal anti-Jewish feeling in the modern world. Consequently, when for some reason or the other it has been desired to encourage Jew-baiting as a popular amusement, it has always been necessary first to make the flesh of the people creep with the repetition of charges against the Jews, generally so absurd that only the fact that the crowd mentality scorns common sense gives them their evil influence.

In his book *Mein Kampf*, first published in 1924 and the last edition of which was issued in 1932, Herr Hitler says: "The Jew to-day is the great instigator of the complete destruction of Germany. Wherever in the world we read attacks on Germany, they are manufactured by Jews, just as in peace times and during the war the Jewish stock exchange and

Marxist press fanned hate against Germany according to plan, until State after State gave up its neutrality.'' That is the sort of stuff with which passion has been inflamed in Germany. The Nazi cause, for what it is worth, involves a complete contradiction. On the one hand von Papen has protested that Jewish predominance in German intellectual, financial and political life had become intolerable. On the other hand, here is Hitler's assertion that the Jews are eager for '' the complete destruction of the country,'' in which, before the Nazi revolution, they had a far greater influence than in any other country in the world. There is no evidence whatever that before, after, or during the war the Jews, either in or outside Germany, were engaged in anti-Teutonic conspiracies. The Jewish financial power in the world would have been clearly increased by a German victory, and it will be remembered that there was a certain not unreasonable suspicion that Jewish financiers in New York, most of them of German origin, used all their influence to prevent American intervention on the side of the Allies.

The reference to the '' Marxist press '' is particularly illuminative of Herr Hitler's complete indifference to facts. ' Marxist' with him is always a very wide term, including Communist, Socialist, and what the Americans call Radical. The Marxist Press includes the *New Statesman*, the *Daily Herald*, and, I suppose, the *Manchester Guardian*. It certainly includes the American *New Republic*, and the Socialist newspapers in France. All these papers have for years urged a

revision of the peace treaties and fair play for
Germany. Far from " fanning hate " they have been
urging understanding and good will. Herr Hitler's
" Marxist press " is by no means controlled by Jews,
but such distinguished Jews as Harold Laski in
England, Walter Lippmann in America, and Leon
Blum in France, have been conspicuous in support of
a more enlightened international policy. From the
beginning to the end there is not one item in Herr
Hitler's indictment capable of proof.

Germany's national pride compelled her to find
some plausible reason for the defeat of 1918. A victim
had to be found, and there was ample precedent for
blaming the Jews. The virulent anti-Semitism of the
past months has been simmering for years, the most
distinguished of its martyrs having been that high-
minded *bourgeois* thinker, Walther Rathenau.

It is alleged that anti-Semitism in Germany is
directed not against the really German Jews, settled
in the country for generations, but against recent
immigrants from Poland and Russia who were
allowed by the Republican Government to settle in the
country. In an article, published in the *Morning Post*
on April 24, 1932, Dr. Ulrich Kahrstedt, Professor of
Ancient History in the University of Göttingen, said:

> German anti-Semitism is not due to any peculiarly cruel
> disposition of German people, but simply to the fact that
> Germany is fifteen degrees of longitude further east than
> England. Germany is practically contiguous with Jewish
> territories to the east, with countries where Polish,
> Russian and Galician Jews live by millions. All the

present difficulties could have been avoided if the German Republic, after 1918, had followed the principle adopted in practically every country in the world which has to deal with immigration, viz. to scrutinize those who wish to cross the frontier and exclude the undesirable. For some fifteen years the German Government, always more or less under ' red ' influences, did everything to encourage eastern immigration. It was practically an Asiatic immigration, bringing in a class of the lowest standard of life, rapidly ruining the middle classes by a competition based on business principles which cannot be adopted by a clean and honest business man of European descent.

The immigrants, who had grown up in ideas hostile to every Government owing to the life they lived under the Tsars, continued their propaganda on German territory. The bookstalls became centres of anti-German propaganda, memoirs of German soldiers who did their duty during the war could hardly find a publisher, and books throwing dirt on everything German, ridiculing everything German, every hero of German history, attacking the memory of every great name of our past, flooded the market. To say nothing of the pornographical productions on the stage and in periodicals, at every corner.

But unfortunately for Dr. Kahrstedt, official statistics suggest that there has been no such devastating immigration. Even if there had been, it is hardly conceivable that " the outcasts of the ghettos of Salonika and Lemberg ", to use his phrase, could have acquired such an immense influence for evil in the course of a dozen years. The truth is that the Jewish population of Germany was higher in 1910 than it was in 1925. From 1890 to 1914 there was a definite immigration of Jews from Russia into

Germany, the numbers growing fewer after the beginning of this century. Since the war the immigration has become a very small dribble, while there has been a large emigration of Jews from Germany to Brazil and the Argentine. So far as I have been able to test the figures, there would seem to have been 80,000 Jewish immigrants into Germany since the war from Russia, Smyrna, and Salonika, and the same number into France.

There is no possible justification in the events of contemporary history for the Nazi anti-Semitism, and it is highly significant that, evidently aware of the flimsiness of the particular charges, the Nazi leaders have revived ancient and utterly discredited general charges against the Jews. The stories of the ritual murders were repeated throughout Germany after the Hitler victory, and there was reasonable apprehension that these fantastic fables might once again have excited outrage and massacre. In Lincoln Cathedral there is the monument of a boy known as Little St. Hugh of Lincoln, said to have been murdered by the Jews of the city—the story is told by Chaucer—as part of the Passover ritual. Jews were continually accused of such ritual murders in the Middle Ages, as the early Christians had been accused of them, and with just as little justification. The Church strongly condemned the accusations, and denunciations of them were published in three Papal Bulls. But there are some lies that never die. In the Russian pogroms at the end of last century the fury of the peasants was aroused by stories of murdered children, and now, forty years later, the fiction crops up again with the same malign purpose.

Little less fantastic and little less wicked is the history of that strange literary curiosity the *Protocols of the Elders of Zion*, a new German edition of which has been published this year. The *Protocols* were first published in Russia in 1905. They were published in French and English in 1920, and supplied the basis of a book *The Jewish Peril*, which has had a considerable sale in this country. They purport to be the notes of a plan for the complete subjugation of the world by the Jews, submitted to the First Zionist Congress in Basle in 1897 by Theodor Hertzl, the founder of the Zionist movement.

I find it difficult to believe that any sane person could take this farrago of nonsense seriously. But monstrous as are the plans with which the Elders are credited, there is considerable ingenuity in the manner of the writer's attempt to excite hostility to the Jews. Thus the *Protocols* are said to have been signed by " Zionist representatives of the 33rd Degree in Orient Freemasonry ". It is unquestionably true that Grand Orient Freemasonry has largely inspired and directed Continental anti-clericalism. This particular form of Freemasonry is—I have no personal knowledge—an entirely different thing from the philanthrophic British variety. Freemasonry is said to have been largely responsible for the French Revolution of 1789, as it may well have been for the *bourgeois* and definitely anti-clerical revolution of 1830. The recent revolution in Spain, again both *bourgeois* and anti-clerical, may have been inspired by Freemasonry, which was certainly powerful in pre-Fascist Italy. But the 1789 story is absurd. No one with any knowledge of the political and social circumstances of the eighteenth century will believe that the Bourbon *régime* could have been destroyed by the members of the secret society, of which Casanova had been a distinguished member, against the will of the French people. But there is reason to believe that the Grand Orient has been, and still is, a powerful middle-class revolutionary society, intent on the establishment of the republican form of government and on the despoilment of the Church, but not, I should suppose, on the destruction of the society that ensures the *bourgeoisie* protection for its bank balances.

Mr. Belloc believes that the Grand Orient is controlled by Jews. He believes, that is, that there is a Jew-directed international campaign against the Church. I do not know on what evidence this belief is based. The endeavour to connect the *Protocols*, the Jews, and the Grand Orient, is important, and the rejection of the charge as the invention of prejudice is justified by the nature of the *Protocols*. In August 1921, *The Times* published three articles by its Constantinople correspondent, in which it was conclusively shown that the *Protocols* are a clumsy plagiarism of a book, written as an attack on the despotism of Napoleon III, by Maurice Joly, a Paris lawyer, and published in Geneva in 1864 with the title *Dialogue aux Enfers entre Machiavel et Montesquieu ou la Politique de Machiavel au XIX Siècle.*

THE JEW TO-DAY

In a leading article in its issue of August 18, 1921, *The Times* said:

> The author of the *Protocols* simply copied from the *Dialogues* a number of passages in which Machiavelli is made to enunciate the doctrines and tactics of despotism as they were at that time practised by Napoleon, and put them into the mouth of an imaginary Jewish Elder. There can be little doubt that the forgery was perpetrated by some member of the Russian Secret Police. . . . For many years there was a close connexion between the Russian and the French police, and one of the confiscated copies of Joly's book may easily have fallen into the hands of a Russian agent—such as Rachkovsky, at one time head of the Russian Secret Police in Paris, to whom other and more clumsy forgeries have been traced—and may have inspired him to invent a weapon for use against Jewish revolutionaries. At any rate the fact of the plagiarism may now be conclusively established and the legend may be allowed to pass into oblivion.

The Times was far too optimistic. Twelve years have passed since it published its leading article, and the legend is still repeated and believed. It has been repeated because it represents the Jews as the secret enemies of Christian society, seeking to ensure its destruction by debauching its morals, and such charges are calculated to have a tremendous effect on the minds of decent men and women, none too intelligent and none too experienced. And in Germany where, until the Hitler revolution, many of the most influential newspapers were notoriously owned and written by Jews, it has been easy to persuade the public that these Jewish newspapers, ostensibly representing different interests and different opinions, engaged together in a secret conspiracy to accentuate hostile feelings between the various sections of the German people and to destroy national solidarity in the manner that the *Protocols* suggest. " These newspapers, like the Indian God Vishnu, will be possessed of hundreds of hands, each of which will be feeling the pulse of varying public opinion."

Here, too, say the Nazi apologists, are Jews making fortunes out of brothels, disreputable night cafés, immoral books ! Read the *Protocols* and you will find it is all according to plan !

The *Protocols* are a fake, and the Hitler leaders must know that they are a fake. That they have used this proved imposture to secure support in their campaign against the Jews makes it reasonable to suppose that they can produce no evidence for their charges and that the charges are entirely untrue.

The *Protocols* were published in 1905, the year of the unsuccessful Russian revolution, which, as Trotsky insists, was the prelude to the revolution of 1917 and made the success of the second revolution possible. *The Times* correspondent writes :

> The Protocols were designed to foster the belief among Russian Conservatives and especially in Court circles, that the prime cause of discontent among the politically-minded elements in Russia was not the repressive policy of the bureaucracy, but a world-wide Jewish conspiracy. They thus served as a weapon against the Russian Liberals, who urged the Tsar to make certain concessions to the *intelligentsia*.

In another place the correspondent says that " a proof of Jewish conspiracy was required as a weapon for the Conservatives against the Liberal elements in Russia ". The intention of the forgery was to persuade " all sorts of mostly well-to-do people that every recent manifestation of discontent on the part of the poor is an unnatural phenomenon, a factitious agitation caused by a secret society of Jews ". This is not quoted from a Jewish apologist or a revolutionary Socialist but from *The Times* newspaper. And the findings are not only a complete condemnation of a vicious publication, but an invaluable suggestion of the origin of modern anti-Semitism.

The medieval hatred of the Jew was the hatred of the borrower for the lender; of the native, often miserably poor, for the alien who was waxing rich. The pogroms in Russia, Rumania, and Poland, at the end of last century and the beginning of this were, to a large extent, a survival of this medieval feeling, and loot, badly needed by the peasantry and the town workers, was the reward of Jew-baiting. These anti-Semitic outbreaks were social and economic in their origin. But the pogroms were tolerated and encouraged by authority whose motive was political. Rome, seething with discontent, was kept quiet with bread and circuses. Russia, on the verge of revolution, was kept quiet by the blood and the possessions of the Jews.

The anti-Semitic outbreak in Russia consisted of a series of massacres in nearly two hundred towns and villages from Warsaw to Odessa. The bureaucrats, who permitted the massacres, were extreme Slavophils, who found or pretended to find in the excesses of the peasants a popular approval of their policy, and, moreover, as I have said, while the proletariat were killing Jews, they were not likely to be interested in a democratic movement which threatened the existence of the autocracy. The pogroms were followed by the passing of a series of laws known as the May Laws which imposed a number of new and rigorous penalties on the Jews, forcing those of them, who were living in villages, into the towns, and imposing various restrictions on them as traders.

The consequence is very interesting. The persecution of the '80's was the beginning of the great trek of Russian and Polish Jews to America and to England, and caused bankers in Berlin and London, owing partly to Jewish influence, but also to Christian indignation, which found its expression in London at great meetings in the Guildhall, to refuse a Russian loan. This compelled the Tsar to negotiate with Paris, and the financial negotiations were the beginning of the Franco-Russian alliance, which has so profoundly affected the history of Europe. Anti-Semitism brought Republican France and Tsarist Russia into a strange bed-fellowship.

If the anti-Semitism of the pogroms appears to be finally political, and the anti-Semitism of the *protocols* is as *The Times* asserts definitely connected with the Russian revolution of 1905, the more recent anti-Semitic movements in Central and Western Europe are still more obviously political. "Anti-Semitism," says Lucien Wolf, "is exclusively a question of European politics, and its origin is to be found, not in the long struggle between Europe and Asia, or between the Church and the Synagogue, which filled so much of ancient and mediæval history, but in the social conditions resulting from the emancipation of the Jews in the middle of the 19th century."

Jewish political emancipation began with the French Revolution. In the League of Nations' debate on the treatment of Jews in Silesia, M. Paul-Boncour, the French Foreign Minister, recalled that it was the traditional policy of the Republic to regard its Jewish citizens as in every respect the equals of its non-Jewish citizens. The emancipated Jew in France and elsewhere was naturally a strenuous supporter of Liberalism. "Twenty centuries of a terrible oppression has made of the Jews in Europe an element of no small importance in all the struggles for popular liberties." Accepting Mr. Christopher Dawson's description of the Jew as the *bourgeois par excellence* it was inevitable that he should be a keen supporter of the *bourgeois* revolution of 1830 as he certainly was of the revolution of 1848, one of the leaders of which the Jew, Louis Boerne, declaring, when chided with his excess of zeal, "I was born a slave and hence I love freedom better than you do." But though the Jews were concerned in all the struggles for popular liberties, they were only rarely among their leaders. They may perhaps have pulled the strings in the secrecy of Masonic lodges, but there is abundant justification for Lucien Wolf's claim that "they have always remained a relatively conservative force ". That is the inevitable consequence of their *bourgeois* attitude of mind.

To estimate the meaning and significance of anti-Semitism as it exists to-day, it is necessary to recall its history in the nineteenth century. The victory of the Germans in 1870 was followed by the swiftly increasing political influence of the industrialists who had, as their political machine, the newly created National Liberal party, among the leaders of which were certain gifted Jews. The influence of the new party was hotly resented by the Prussian agrarians, and the clash between industrialists and agrarians— between the flamboyant and the drab—caused a serious financial crisis in 1873. The trouble was attributed to Jewish malevolence in a widely-circulated pamphlet called "Victory of Judaism over Germanism", in which many of Herr Hitler's extravagances were anticipated. The National Liberals had supported Bismarck's *Kulturkampf* policy, and this caused the German Roman Catholics to support the anti-Semitic movement which went on steadily during the '70's.

Incidentally it is interesting to note the general attitude of the Roman Church to the Jewish problem. In the Middle Ages, as I have said, Popes denounced the ritual murder charges, though Jews were among the victims of the Inquisition. In modern times the Vatican has sternly condemned Jew-baiting, but, during the past fifty years, the Roman Church, both in Germany and in France, has supported anti-

Semitic agitations. In America Jews and Roman
Catholics were equally anathema to the Klu-Klux-
Klan. In Germany since the war, they were allied in
the endeavour, in face of appalling difficulty, to estab-
lish their country as a progressive republic, and if the
Weimar Constitution was the creation of a Socialist
Jew, the ablest of the constitutional statesmen was the
Catholic Dr. Brüning. The Jew in Germany to-day is
a helot. The power of the Clerical Centre is broken.
But between Berlin and the Vatican there is peace.

To return to my story. In 1879, Bismarck, who had
hitherto consistently opposed anti-Semitism, quarrelled
with the National Liberal party and deliberately fanned
anti-Semitic prejudice which found its pseudo-
philosophic defender in the historian, Treitschke.
Treitschke was a pupil of Hegel, and he taught the
doctrine that a nation should be a definite coherent
unit, consisting of men of the same race and the same
religion. In later times, this doctrine was developed by
Houston Chamberlain, who had read and only
partially understood Gobineau and Nietzsche, in his
notorious *Foundations of the Nineteenth Century*, the
book which did so much to inflame German national
ambition in the years before the war.

In the '80's anti-Semitism in Germany was fanned
into a new life by Adolf Stocker, one of the Court
chaplains. There was rioting in the streets of many
cities with the familiar maltreating of harmless " non-
Aryans ", and it was proposed, in the Prussian Diet,
to shut the Jews out of high schools and universities
as they have now been shut out by Herr Hitler's

decrees. The anti-Semitic proposals were supported by the parties of the Right and the Centre and resisted, with considerable success, by the Liberals, who had the outspoken support of the Crown Prince and the Crown Princess, afterwards the Emperor and Empress Frederick.

For a while German anti-Semitism had a set-back. The conscience of the nation was revolted by the Russian pogroms, and its common sense outraged by the repetition in Hungary of the ancient charges against the Jews of ritual murder. In 1894, by the way, a German Roman Catholic priest—the Catholics at this time were as vehement as the Lutherans in their denunciation of the Jews—was prosecuted and sent to gaol for repeating the Blood Accusation. But anti-Semitism remained inherent in the anti-Liberal parties, and so late as 1892 the Conservatives, while officially repudiating anti-Semitism, declared that one of their objects was to '' combat the oppressive and disintegrating Jewish influence on our national life ''.

The Hohenzollerns were definitely opposed to anti-Semitism. Frederick III described it as '' the scandal of the century ''. His son, the ex-Kaiser Wilhelm—I quote Emil Ludwig—'' made Dernburg his minister and Ballin his minister ''. And Ballin, more than any other man, was responsible for the emergence of Germany as the active rival of Great Britain in the traffic of the seas.

There was little obvious anti-Semitism in Germany in the years before the war, but it is a fact to be remembered as showing the continuance of Jewish interest in "the struggles for popular liberties" that half the members of the Social Democratic Party, that very cautious *bourgeois* party in the pre-war Reichstag, were Jews.

I must return to the last century. In none of its incidents is the essential political character of anti-Semitism more clear than in the *affaire Dreyfus*. *Bourgeois* France had accepted the penalties of the defeat of 1870 with courage and resignation. The war indemnity was paid with a promptness that astonished and disconcerted Bismarck, and the Third Republic, *bourgeois* and Freemason, set itself to repair what the giddy irresponsibility of the Third Empire had destroyed. But a section of young France, Royalist and Catholic in sentiment, excited by the preaching of *la revanche* by the poet, Paul Deroulède, was impatient of the humdrum resignation of the Republican Government and eagerly backed General Boulanger, the most pinchbeck of adventurers, in his anti-Republican, or it would be more correct to say his anti-*bourgeois* campaign, again the flamboyant revolting against the drab. In 1888, Boulanger was a popular idol, the hero of a well known song *En Revenant de la Révue*, sung by Paulus, the most famous of all French *lions comiques*, and if he had had an ounce of pluck, he might have marched on the Palais Elysée on July 14 and have destroyed the Republic. But Boulanger failed his supporters, and Boulangerism was destroyed by a Jewish statesman—Joseph Reinach.

There followed the Panama scandals, in which three Jews, one of whom was Reinach's uncle, were concerned, and a raging, tearing anti-Semitic agitation began in France, led by Edouard Drumont, who, it was said, was himself partly Jewish, in his paper *La Libre Parole*. The Jew was the enemy. It was the Jew who was preventing France from once again attaining her proper position in Europe—again, almost in every detail, the anticipation of Hitler. And again the Jew was attacked, mainly because he was the *bourgeois par excellence*.

In the midst of the Drumont agitation, Alfred Dreyfus, a Jewish artillery officer, on the staff of the *Ministère de la Guerre*, was arrested on the charge of betraying military secrets to Germany. Dreyfus is one of the tragic figures of the later nineteenth century, and guilty or not guilty, he was a pawn in a political game. The French army had remained, in its higher commands, anti-Republican and Catholic. The Government, realizing the danger to the Republic after the Boulanger conspiracy, set out to introduce good anti-Clerical Republicans into the War Office, and Dreyfus was broken in the struggle between the two parties, he, of course, being an anti-Clerical. There are, I suppose, few foreigners familiar with the famous trials who have much doubt that Dreyfus was innocent. There is still a considerable number of Frenchmen who are convinced of his guilt. To me it is remarkable that, supposing the Clerical-Conservative party in the War Office saw in Dreyfus's alleged offences the opportunity to pillory their opponents as enemies of the Fatherland, they did not make surer of the evidence before they moved. Dreyfus belonged to a wealthy and influential family. He could rely on a first-rate defence. If he could be proved guilty, both Republicans and Jews would be hopelessly discredited. But if, even after years—and this is what actually happened—the prosecution failed, it must prove a grave political blunder. The guilt or innocence of Alfred Dreyfus was a political issue. The parties of the Left, the Radicals and Socialists, were certain that he was innocent, but mainly because the parties of the Right were certain that he was guilty.

When, after years of suffering, Dreyfus was rehabilitated, the Left won a great victory, and a definite anti-Clerical bias was given to French politics, a bias which resulted in the breaking of the Concordat with Rome by the Combes government.

It is to be regretted that anti-Semitism should appear to be pitted against anti-Clericalism as the two main developments of a nation's politics, and it is not to be denied that the Church made a costly blunder when it associated itself with anti-Semitism in France.

There is a footnote to the *affaire Dreyfus* which I cannot refrain from writing. When the great test of the war came, the Republican-Freemason generals to whom, as a consequence of the Conservative-Clerical rout, almost all the high commands had fallen, almost all failed, and France was ultimately saved by the soldiers of the Right. Such is the irony of history!

We pass on to the Russian revolution of 1905 and the publication of *The Protocols of the Elders of Zion*. It was natural that the Jews in Russia should have associated themselves with the attempt to establish

32

a Liberal *régime*. No other Russians had suffered so severely and so persistently from the cruelties of the Tsarist rule. But even in Russia, what Lucien Wolf has called the Jews' "innate moderation" prevented them from being concerned with the campaigns of violence, and the only connexion of the Jews with Nihilist outrages was the trial of a Jewess in whose house one of the plots had been hatched. They, however, supplied a considerable proportion of the brains and drive of the more moderate agitation. Lucien Wolf says: "As early as 1885 the Jewish workmen, assisted by Jewish university students, led the way in the formation of Trades Unions. They also became the *colporteurs* of western European Socialism, and they played an important part in the organisation of the Russian Social Democratic Federation, which their Arbeiter-Bund joined in 1898 with no fewer than 30,000 members. The Revolutionary organisation was partly Jewish. It was the intention of the Russian Government to make it seem that it was entirely Jewish—a foreign plot to lure ingenuous Russians into revolt against the Little Father."

The Jew has ever been of immense service to the reactionary. He has enabled him to assert that every Liberal movement is foreign, that Conservatism and patriotism are synonymous terms, that the nation would be quite happy under its native oppressors if it were not for the malevolent whisperings of alien agitators. In Germany, in France, in Russia, pre-war anti-Semitism was anti-Liberalism.

The Russian revolution of 1917 is the beginning of

a new chapter in the history of anti-Semitism. The successful establishment of the Bolshevist rule in Russia is certainly the most startling event in modern history, and will probably prove to be the most portentous. While incompetent soldiers were still capering and voluble politicians were proving (to the peoples' undoing) that they were not and never could be statesmen, a little scrubby undistinguished man suddenly appeared, without heralding his coming, on the centre of the European stage. He was the most dangerous of all men, a man with ideas, and circumstances gave him an unprecedented opportunity for putting his ideas into practice. Lenin was not a Jew. But he was the apostle of Marxian social philosophy, and Karl Marx was a Jew by race. Consequently for the past sixteen years Bolshevism has been presented to a bewildered and very nervous world as the latest, most complete, and most menacing, of Jewish plots against Christian civilization; and every outbreak of anti-Semitism is excused on the ground that it is really anti-Bolshevist.

In his book *The Jewish Bogey* (p. 19) Lucien Wolf says:

The appeal to Karl Marx as the Archetype of the Jewish Revolutionist is, in this connection, particularly unfortunate. In the first place, Marx was not even remotely a Jew by religion, and therefore the Messianic motive is scarcely likely to have weighed with him. He was probably a sincere Revolutionist, and, in that case, he was just as little a Jew, seeing that his philosophy has no relation to any recognised school of Jewish thought. Marx, indeed, was an intellectual product of the essentially Gentile teachings of Hegel and Feuerbach.

This is not very convincing. If only Jews, who are religious, are to be regarded as Jews, then three-quarters of intellectual Jewry will be Gentilized. No one, I should suppose, has ever charged Marx with himself being affected by a Messianic motive, even though his *Das Kapital* may have become the Bible—the much-annotated Bible—of a new religion. As to the suggestion that the Marxian philosophy has "no relation to any recognized school of Jewish thought", this assumes that there remains in the world a philosophy and a culture that are distinctively Jewish, and I propose to dispose of this claim in a separate chapter.

Karl Marx, Lenin's master, and Trotsky, Lenin's most gifted lieutenant, were Jews, and it was not altogether unreasonable to regard Bolshevism as Jewish, and to confuse Jews and Bolshevists. That is the intention of *The Jewish Peril*, in which is printed the English translation of *The Protocols*. That is the excuse for the Nazi policy of repression. As I say, it is not to be dismissed as altogether reasonless. Nothing is more dangerous than to conclude that one's opponents have no case simply because their proceedings seem reasonless or immoral. For a great part of my own time I am concerned with the defence of a certain dogmatic view of the character and life of men which is being insistently and intelligently attacked in these days as it has never been attacked before. And it is evident that such defence is impossible if what to me are subversive writings are put, unread, on an *Index Expurgatorium*, and without the recognition of the intelligence of the attack. Similarly with anti-Semitism, it is impolitic to attribute every outbreak to the evil in the Gentile heart, as it is unwise to exaggerate the extent of what is, however modified it may be, a scandalous iniquity. To overstate a case is often to lose a case.

Nothing but harm is done by such statements as the following which I quote from Lewis Browne's *The Story of the Jews* (p. 294): " All the forces of reaction everywhere let loose after the war, turned with the old venom upon the Jew. Wherever custom made it possible, he was starved and murdered; everywhere else he was reviled and despised." In both what they actually state and what they imply these two sentences are mischievously untrue. It is true that the Poles misused their recovered freedom by persecution of the Jews—"wholesale massacres ", Mr. Browne's term, is a gross exaggeration—and also of the members of the Orthodox Church. It is not true that in west Europe, the Jew, who had done his part in the war, was "reviled and despised ". In Hungary, the fact that an abortive Bolshevist revolution was led by a Jew, Bela Kuhn, certainly encouraged anti-Semitism in that country, while there was some excuse for regarding the ruthless persecution of Christians in Russia—a persecution every bit as thorough and brutal as that of the Jews in Germany—with the organized blasphemous travesties of Christian worship, as the work of the " Elders of Zion " as, in the eyes of the world, Trotsky was responsible with Lenin for the direction of Bolshevist policy, and the persecutions were actually directed by another Jew, Zinovieff.

I have no sort of doubt that, if every Jew in Europe had been exterminated before 1917, the Bolshevist revolution would still have occurred, and would have proceeded as it has actually proceeded. It is not surprising that Jews were found among the Bolshevists. " Human nature being what it is," says Lucien Wolf, " it would not have been surprising if all the Jews in Russia had become fanatical Bolsheviks. The extravagances of Bolshevism are the natural reaction against the cruelties of Tsarism, and the Jews suffered more bitterly from these cruelties than any other section of the sorely tried Russian people." But to hold Jewry responsible for Bolshevism is ridiculous.

With regard to this gigantic politico-social experiment, Jews are as divided as they are about everything else. Harold Laski is, perhaps, the most considerable apologist of Bolshevism outside Russia; but another Jew, Fulop Müller, is among its most effective critics. Still, in the circumstances of the times, the Jew can hardly be surprised if the general and natural fear of Bolshevism finds its expression in a more or less vague anti-Semitism, this being another proof that anti-Semitism is political.

Before the Hitler victory, the Germany of big and little business, of the farmer and the pious peasant, lived in dread of a general Communist rising. The majority of the men and women, who voted for the

Nazis, knew and cared nothing for Aryans and non-Aryans, and were not particularly anti-Jewish. But they had seen the Communists growing stronger and more arrogant, and they had learned that the Reich governors, depending on the support of the Catholic Centre and the Socialists, were unable to destroy the Red Peril. Hitler rules in Berlin mainly from the German fear of Moscow. I have been unable to obtain anything like reliable information concerning the German Communist Party, but I am told by English sympathizers with Communism that it probably counts a considerable number of young Jews among its members, sufficient anyhow for the familiar pretence that Communism is not a native revolutionary movement, inspired by hatred of existing social conditions, but an artificial movement fomented by alien enemies of the Fatherland.

The defence for the attacks on the Jews is that they are revolutionaries, though it is certain that of the 600,000 Jews in Germany not more than two or three per cent have any Communist sympathy. To the Nazi there is no difference between Socialists and Communists. They even go further and denounce all their opponents as sympathizers with Moscow. Thus Dr. Kahrstedt describes the Governments of Stresemann and Brüning as "more or less Red"! If the Jew is not a Communist, the Nazis assume that he is a Socialist, which is just as bad. And, anyway, he is a Jew!

Jew-baiting is part of the official Nazi programme, and despite the protests from Geneva and everywhere else, it is being carried out according to plan. It has been often said, and it would be pleasant to believe, that the persecutors of the Jews have always paid dearly for their wickedness. " The Jews ", Dean Inge said recently, " have stood by the graves of all their oppressors in turn." But they were driven out of England by Edward I; they were driven out of the Rhine Valley after the Black Death; they were driven out of Spain by Ferdinand and Isabella. And they may well be starved out of modern Germany, or left to live there as helots with no citizen rights, constantly at the mercy of jealous ' Christian ' neighbours and of every petty blackmailing policeman. That must be the fate of the German Jew if the Hitler fantastic ambition of a Germany inhabited by " a hundred per cent Germans " (a large number will inevitably have Slav, Jewish and other alien blood in their veins) is to be realized.

There is one particular reason for German anti-Semitism. The German is afraid of the Jew. So is the Pole. In Poland the Jews are ten per cent of the population, and there is very insistent fear of Jewish competition, both in commerce and in the professions. The rights of the Jewish minority were supposed to be guaranteed by the Treaty of Versailles, but the Polish Government has been as ingenious as the Rumanian Government in getting round the treaty obligations. The Government suppresses acts of violence, and the Jews are not deprived of citizen rights. There were, some few years ago, thirty-five Jewish deputies in the Polish Parliament, and there

are still ten. But the Jew has to pay for his few
privileges. Only one-fourth of the Polish population
is urban, and a third of the urban population is
Jewish. The town population supplies more than half
the national revenue, and it is estimated that the
Jews, ten per cent of the population, pay between
twenty and thirty per cent of the state taxes. It is
made immensely difficult for the young Jew to obtain
entry into the state technical schools. There is a
definite and very small Jewish quota in all the
universities. There are hardly any Jews in the public
services. There is dire distress among the poor Jews
of the towns, some of it due to the world crisis, some
of it due to state and municipal discrimination.
Poland has, indeed, shown Hitler the way. As a
Jewish journalist recently wrote: "With an elaborate
system for impoverishing, degrading, demoralising,
and crushing the Jews, why should the Polish
Government be in favour of physical attacks? It
can achieve its purpose more subtly and securely by
enactments and administrative regulations, and it can
enjoy the reputation of being a respectable Government that is opposed to pogroms."

The Jews are only one per cent of the German
population. They are three-quarters of one per cent
of the population of Great Britain. In this country
I find that considerably fewer than a hundred Jews
(say point-one per cent of the Jewish population) are
conspicuous figures in the national life—in politics,
finance, commerce, the professions, and the arts. In
Germany it is a Nazi complaint that not only in

finance but in the university faculties, in medicine and surgery, in journalism and the arts, the Jews have an intolerable predominance. It is, indeed, the fact that the Jew has mattered more in Germany than in any other country in the world, possibly more than in all the other countries in the world counted together. In music Bruno Walther carries on the great German-Jewish tradition. Three German-Jewish chemists and three German-Jewish physicists (Einstein being one of them) have been Nobel prize-winners, and it must not be forgotten that it is only since the war that Jews have been allowed to hold professorships in the German universities. Hermann Aron was one of the pioneers of wireless telegraphy; Abraham Stern invented the calculating machine; Karl Arenstein built the zeppelin that crossed the Atlantic in 1924. In medicine, the name of Paul Erlich comes at once to the mind; and German-Jewish consulting physicians are famous all through Europe. The great German banks, the Darmstater Bank, the Dresden Bank and the Berliner Hoedels-gesellschafter were Jewish enterprises; and there is a certain irony in the fact that Dr. Schacht, the Nazi-appointed President of the Reichbank, learned his trade from the Jews.

Why have the Jews been so important in Germany? I have considered various answers to this question. Emil Ludwig has suggested that the German and the Jew are much alike in their mental and spiritual qualities (which I do not think is true), and that, therefore, the Jewish genius has flowered most successfully in a German environment. The German universities, with the possibility of a liberal education, were open to Jews many years before they were admitted to Oxford and Cambridge, and the German Jew has, therefore, a tradition of culture that few English Jews possess. More important, in this connexion, it must be remembered that while probably the majority of Jews in England have not been here for more than three generations—I am assured that not half a dozen of the families of the Cromwell re-settlement remain—and certainly the majority of Jews in America are only in the second generation, a large percentage of the Jews in Germany have been in the country for centuries. The German Jew is far more German than the English Jew is English.

These facts explain to some extent the Jew's prominence in the life of Germany, but they do not altogether explain why his importance is so much greater in Germany than in England. The truth is that the Germans are a stupid people. In his book, *Germany Puts the Clock Back*, Edgar Mowrer says of the Germans that they are " rich in intellect, poor in common sense ". On the other hand, the English still possess a considerable dowry of common sense. It is a familiar *cliché* that the old Germany of the Meistersingers has been succeeded by a Germany of hard-headed business men. But Germany, as its recent history makes quite clear, is still a nation of sentimentalists, ready to be beguiled by blessed words and blessed phrases, and sentimentalists are always stupid. The Jew is rarely sentimental and stupid, and pitted against the German in the schools and the professions, the prizes fall to him as a matter of course. A distinguished Oxford professor, with a cosmopolitan experience that few dons can claim, tells me that he has been surprised to find how rarely the Jewish undergraduates in English universities are conspicuously distinguished among their fellows. On the whole, they are rather above the average. But that is all. And it is really very little when it is remembered that many young Jews go to the universities with scholarships and are the picked men of their tribe. " The English and the French ", a Jewish scholar has said, " are quite as intelligent as we are, and all we can do in England and France is to be content with very occasional distinction. The Scottish are far more intelligent than we are. But in Germany we can fairly claim a definitely higher average of intelligence."

The author of *The International Jew*, that futile American essay in anti-Semitism, declares that the Jew particularly hates the German. But why should he? No boxer hates the opponent whom he can knock out in the first round. But the German dislikes the Jew because he has good reason to fear him. He has the common attitude of the half-competent to the very competent; of the boy who, try hard as he may, can never go higher than fifth in his class, to the boy who is always top. Jewish distinction excites envy, and envy and jealousy can easily be excited into venomous hatred.

Suppose that, in England, fat briefs in important

43

cases went as a matter of course to Jewish barristers, then the Jew would certainly not be loved in the Temple. Suppose that Jewish surgeons were generally called in for important and well-paid operations, and that Harley Street bristled with the plates of Jewish consulting physicians, then it is certain that angry letters from less successful Gentile practitioners would be regularly addressed to the editor of the *British Medical Journal*. Suppose that the editors of the more important English newspapers were Jews, and that Jews held most of the influential positions on their staffs, then there would be constant anti-Semitic murmuring in the Press Club. That is the position in Germany. The Jew is too successful, and he is paying the price for success. Lawyers, doctors, and journalists probably had little part in the hooligan outrages, but they are naturally eager supporters of the Hitler policy of driving their competitors out of the field.

The consideration of the present position in Germany would seem to suggest some modification of Lucien Wolf's contention that anti-Semitism is political and that the Jew is attacked because he is a Liberal. But that is at least part of the truth. To it, in Germany, is to be added a widespread dislike of the Jew, not because he is a 'non-Aryan', nor because, when he worships God at all, he worships Him in a synagogue and not in a church, but because he is too clever. It is easy to persuade the struggling doctor, angling in vain for patients, with a string of waiting cars outside the consulting-room of a

Jewish competitor, that Germany would be a far happier country if it were inhabited entirely by ' Aryans '.

There is a definite connexion, probably rarely apprehended, between anti-Semitism and the reaction against democracy that is one of the most important world movements of the past few years. I am certain that economic causes have a far smaller effect on human history than appears to be generally believed. If the Treaties had been modified, and Germany had been assisted to industrial recovery while, at the same time, a position of equality among the nations had been granted her, the Hitler revolution might never have occurred. But there is another and a less material explanation for the triumph of Hitlerism. Discontent with incompetent and corrupt parliamentary government, with fear of the Communism that had broken out in Turin and Milan, made Mussolini's triumphant march to Rome a possibility—these things and something more. Contemporary anti-democratic movements are really anti-*bourgeois* movements, a revolt against *bourgeois* ideals. They are the expressions of the love of the romantic and the picturesque common to most men when they are young. They are, as I said at the beginning of this chapter, a movement of the flamboyant against the tyranny of the drab. They are the rejection by the inexperienced of all that the experienced have learned from the war. " Patriotism is not enough ", said Nurse Cavell, who paid for her patriotism with her life. " The love of country is the most exalted of all human emotions ",

45

is the slogan of the Fascists. While middle-aged statesmen are, with halting hesitation, endeavouring at Geneva to educate the nations to an internationalism that will save the world from war, youth in Italy, and now in Germany (with youth in France by no means unsympathetic), jeers at internationalism as a weak feminist dream, and extols the virtues of war, after the manner of the late Lord Birkenhead in his notorious Glasgow University Rectorial address, and as if the events of 1914-1918 had never occurred. Mussolini inflames his followers by recalling the glories of ancient Rome. Ludendorf would have Germany throw overboard the insipid Christian virtues and return to the worship of Odin and Thor.

The burning of the books in Berlin was a highly significant business on account of the books that were burned. Jews were lumped together on the *Index*— Emil Ludwig, a facile and much over-rated writer whose book on Christ is unpleasant, but who can hardly be regarded as a revolutionary influence; Fulop Müller, whose *Mind and Soul of Bolshevism* is perhaps the most damaging criticism of Communism in practice that has yet been published; Walther Rathenau. And with them not only the authors of Socialist and Communist literature, but the writers of the many striking books that have appeared in modern Germany telling the truth (as all men, who experienced it, know) of the utter beastliness of war; and with them, too, Freud and other exponents of the new psychology, which I happen to regard as most pernicious nonsense. To tell the truth about war is to be a ' defeatist '. To be unorthodox is to be disloyal. To the flames with them all ! Back to Odin and Thor !

To the drab *bourgeois* mind it is all theatrical and absurd. But the theatrical is not always absurd, for man is a histrionic animal. There is deep spiritual significance in his delight in " dressing up ", and there is acute political wisdom in the exploitation of his love for the histrionic. When Mussolini put his Fascists into black shirts, he had taken the first step to victory. I think it was the *New Statesman* that pointed out that conventional " summer shirtings " have no chance against the *chemise noire*. The emblems, the shirts, the classic salutes are the trappings of the new Quixotism, which is sick of the hesitations and drabness, and demands colour and romance. Mussolini can guide and check the movement which he created. Can Hitler ?

It is clear that the *bourgeoisie* is in greater peril from the post-war spiritual reaction to the banner of Thor and the *fasces* of the lictors than it ever was from social *democracy*, since the spiritual ideals of the *bourgeois* and the Socialists are equally humdrum.

In many respects the most significant political adventure of the times is Mr. De Valera's attempt to construct in Southern Ireland a self-dependent Catholic democracy. The economists insist that the prosperity, and consequently, it may be assumed, the happiness of the world, depend on unrestricted buying and selling. Increase the volume of trade, we are told, and international problems will be solved. To Mr. De Valera, buying and selling, in the modern sense, are an altogether immoral business; and the Catholic sociologist will certainly agree with him.

" Produce to sell " says the *bourgeois*. " Produce to consume" says Mr. De Valera; "grow food for your family and your neighbours to eat: weave cloth and make boots for them to wear: build houses for them to live in: don't worry your heads about foreign trade and all the mumbo-jumboism of foreign exchanges: keep your eyes on the village pump and be content if it supplies you with an adequate supply of clear water!" England does not count any more in Southern Ireland, and the Irish Government is intent on destroying—it has not yet been very successful—in Irish towns and villages those *bourgeois* qualities that it regards as characteristically English and therefore detestable.

What Mr. De Valera is attempting in Ireland, Herr Hitler is attempting in Germany on a larger scale, and in face of far greater difficulties. The Irish delegate at Geneva was able, whole-heartedly, to take the lead in condemning the persecution of Jews in Silesia, since there are very few Jews in County Cork. But if the English in Southern Ireland had appealed to the League as a misused minority, they would certainly not have been without a case.

Both De Valera and Hitler must, of course, be dismissed as ignorant, if the social-political maxims, generally accepted since the war, are reliable. The nations are mutually dependent! The prosperity of one depends on the prosperity of them all! Wars must cease, armies must be disbanded, and international

48

disputes must be decided according to international law, in the calm atmosphere of an international court! The ideal, admirable as it is, is *bourgeois*. So are the premises. Are nations mutually dependent? Does the prosperity of one necessarily depend on the prosperity of them all? Mr. De Valera does not believe that they are. Nor, I think, does Signor Mussolini.

Under his rule, Italy has become an anti-*bourgeois* State. Prices and wages are determined by the State experts. Imports and exports are regulated according to the official estimate of the nation's needs. The employer may not discharge a workman, nor the workman change his master, without official permission. The function of Italy is to nourish Italians, the business of Italians is to serve Italy, and in order to serve it effectively in the field, the workshop, and, may be, the army, they must cultivate self-control and self-denial.

It is possible that Fascism may fritter out into chaos. If it secures permanence in Italy, it will probably establish itself throughout Central Europe, and it may affect the Government and the social structure of France and, more unlikely, of Great Britain. My point is that, permanent or ephemeral, Fascism is anti-*bourgeois* and therefore, since the Jew is the *bourgeois par excellence*, to a degree anti-Semitic. It is true that Mussolini warmly repudiates anti-Semitism and that, provided that he is a loyal Fascist, the Jew suffers from no handicap in Italy. But there are few Jews in Italy, and it is difficult to understand how a

Jew can be a good Fascist without losing his Judaism. The loss of all kind of freedom must outrage his centuries-long tradition as a trader. How can the *bourgeois par excellence* tolerate the trading restrictions of a Fascist State?

Fascism demands the idolatrous worship of the State. It is not content with the easy loyalty demanded of its citizens by Great Britain, where " conscientious objection ", based may be on religious convention, to the commands of the State was respected even in the troubled and hectic atmosphere of war. In the Fascist State there is no God but Caesar, and in every Fascist State the Jew would sooner or later be in the position in which he is in to-day in Germany.

Human society is in flux. The old order has come to an end. Some sort of new order is coming into being. It may be the new romantic, sabre-rattling, exaggerated nationalism. And that nationalism must of necessity be anti-Semitic.

The probable alternative is the Communist State, modelled more or less on Bolshevist Russia. How will the Jew fare in such a state? The answer is obviously unaffected by the fact that half a dozen Jews were among the artificers of the Russian revolution, and that to-day there is a considerable number of Jews among the minor Soviet officials. The Communist State resembles the Fascist State in demanding from its citizens unqualified obedience and in the stern restriction of personal liberty. If other Communist States followed Russia—and I agree that in this particular it is quite likely that they may not—the Jew will be compelled to shed his religion as the price of citizenship, and while the Jew may have little fear of persecution under Communism (supposing that he does not practise his religion) he may, in the peculiar conditions, be assimilated in two or three generations. But the Jew is very tough, and however circumstances may change, he always finds means of adapting himself to them, and he has even contrived to maintain his separatism in Soviet Russia. In his *Jewish Life in Modern Times* (p. 141) Mr. Israel Cohen says:

> The Government has allowed the Jews in localities in which they form a majority of the population to form their own Soviets, with Yiddish as the official language in schools and courts, and at the beginning of 1927 there were already 150 such Jewish Soviets, of which 130 were in the Ukraine alone. The motives prompting this apparent generosity may be sought partly in the desire to offer the Jews some compensation for the repression of their religious life, and partly in the wish to deflect Jewish national aspirations from Palestine to self-governing communities in the Ukraine.

But that Communism is necessarily destructive of Jewish separatism, and that the existence of the Jews as a race apart is impossible in a Communist State, is admitted by Jewish writers by no means unsympathetic with the Communist experiment. In an article in the *Jewish Review*, Mr. Harry Sacher says that in the years from 1924 to 1929, one hundred and seventy-eight synagogues were closed in the Ukraine alone, and that the surviving synagogues are in a dilapidated condition, while the teaching of Hebrew and the Jewish religion is made almost impossible. The barriers between Jew and non-Jew are melting away. There is a vast increase of marriages between Jew and non-Jew. Mr. Sacher goes on: "If one were a pessimist one might question whether thirty years from now much more than a remnant of Jewry will survive in Russia. . . . The practical annihilation of Russian Jewry and the extinction of the influence it has exerted on the masses of Jews throughout the world for centuries are eventualities highly probable and not remote."

If the loss of his religion is eventually to mean the disappearance of the Jews as a separatist community, the disappearance of the family as an institution must assuredly lead to the same end, and the family is incompatible with a Communist civilization. The Soviet ambassador to Norway has written:

> The old form of the family is passing away; the *bourgeois* world celebrated the isolation, the cutting off of the married pair from the collective weal; in the scattered and disjointed *bourgeois* society full of struggle and destruction, the family was the sole anchor of hope in the storms of life, the peaceful haven in the ocean of hostilities and competitions between persons. The family represented an individual class in the social unit. There can and must be no such thing in the Communist society. For Communist society as a whole represents such a fortress in the collective life, precluding any possibility of the existence of an isolated class of family bodies, existing by itself, with its ties of birth, its love of family honour, its absolute segregation.

52

Communism, as a system of society must remain *antipathique* to the Jews' tradition and to his sense of values. Disraeli declared that Jews were ineradicably attached to religion and property. The attachment to religion may sit lightly on them in these days; the attachment to property certainly remains. The Jew does not, as a rule, suffer from the lust of possession, but he immensely values the protection of possession. In this again he is the *bourgeois*, but in this, too, he is, to an extent, the heir of the civilization of the Middle Ages. It would seem, therefore, that the only society in which Jew and Judaism can be safe is a society in which personal liberty and personal property are safe. It is an axiom of Catholic sociology that personal liberty cannot be assured, without the possession of personal property or at least, of the possibility of acquiring it. The property-less man has precious little liberty either in England or in America, but the possibility that he may, by some extraordinary freak of fortune, acquire property gives him the shadow of liberty. The Irish sweepstake may be the road to freedom.

A genuinely free community is a community where every one possesses something, and no one possesses too much. The Jew, the super-*bourgeois*, must naturally be inclined to defend things as they are. But the Jew, because of his intelligence, must realize that things cannot remain as they are. Under both Communism and Fascism, he must, as a separate entity, disappear. The only world safe for Judaism is a world in which, while vast modifications are made in the

E   53

social structure and there is a newer and finer conception of values, individual freedom and personal property remain!

I am fearful that such a world—it is the world in which I hope my children's children will live—will be a drab world, far drabber than a Fascist State, less drab than a Bolshevist State. But it is the only world in which the Jew can be safe.

CHAPTER 2

THE QUALITIES OF THE JEW

If I needed some one striking and dramatic evidence of the supernatural and supra-rational direction of the universe, I should find it in the continuance of the Jews, with and yet not with, of and yet not of, the peoples among whom they live. On the face of it there is every reason, political, social and economic, why the Jews should have been assimilated, and after assimilation, should have disappeared with the Phœnicians, the Assyrians, and other races of the ancient world. Actually they have survived the Greeks, because the modern Greeks are infinitely more Slavonic than Hellene. It is a matter of enormous difficulty—indeed, I find it impossible—to explain why they have continued, except that the Jews have suffered as no other people has suffered at the hands of their enemies, that it is eternally true that the Church is watered by the blood of its martyrs, and that the more a nation or a race, or even a sect, is persecuted, the more persistently it continues.

The Jew is the human paradox. The fact of his continuance is conclusive proof that he has a superiority complex, for without such a complex, continuance would have been impossible. For the Jew

55

living among a majority that has frequently harried
him and has nearly always despised him, life has been
made endurable only because he has been persuaded
that he is the elect of God, spiritually and mentally
the superior of the peoples among whom he lives.
But with this superiority complex, there is an equally
persistent inferiority complex. As a distinguished
Jewish journalist said to me recently, when a Jew is
introduced to a non-Jewish acquaintance, he instinctively wonders whether he is disliked or suspected
because of his race. That is the heritage of persecution.

Nearly all generalizations about the qualities of
races and nations are not only inexact, but are the
antitheses of the facts. The English and the French,
who are next-door neighbours, still cherish the most
amazing illusions about each other's characteristics.
Even the experiences of the war were not sufficient to
persuade the French that the English are not a dour,
hard people. Similarly, the illusion continues in
England that the French are generally trivial and
immoral, when the fact is that they are the most
serious, industrious, thrifty people on the face of the
earth, with a love of family only equalled by the Jews.
We have the same kind of misjudgment of the minority
who speak our language, share our responsibilities,
vote in the same polling-booths and live in the next
houses, but who are, to an extent, separate from us by
the possession of an alien tradition and by the stubborn
cherishing of differences, which, when they are dispassionately examined, appear of comparatively small
importance.

56

THE QUALITIES OF THE JEW

There are certain popular and generally accepted conceptions of the Jewish character which do not bear five minutes' examination. Few of what are considered Jewish qualities are common to most Jews, and none of them common to all Jews. Indeed the first conclusion forced on the inquirer into the qualities of the Jew is that the type is so varied, and the individual qualities so different, that it is impossible to discover definite qualities which all Jews, or even most Jews, possess and which few people who are not Jews ever possess. I ask myself, for example, what one spiritual attribute three English Jews of my acquaintance—Mark Hambourg, Harold Laski, and Herbert Samuel—have in common, and I suggest that unless that question can be satisfactorily answered, the suggestion that the Jew, wherever he lives, is a man apart, is entirely untenable. Sir Herbert Samuel appears to me to have the mind and the outlook on life of a cultured English Nonconformist. Lord Riddell, generally an acute judge of his fellow men, says that Sir Herbert Samuel is "usually rather like an Oriental statesman". The comparison seems to me fantastic. No one surely would find anything Oriental in Sir Herbert—(he will, I hope, forgive me for using him as a type, as he is well known in English public life)—and if he were not a Jew, neither Lord Riddell nor anyone else would find anything Eastern in his English middle-class caution and love of compromise. Actually it is as forced to regard Sir Herbert as an Oriental, because his very remote ancestors emigrated from the Holy Land, as it would be to discover common qualities between Herr Hitler, the apostle of " the pure Aryan " and the Grand Llama because the Aryans trekked to Europe from Tibet.

In the modern world, in which most of the men who were rich a few years ago are now much poorer, and the men who were poor are for the most part poorer still, the Jews are notable in the very narrow circle of the *nouveaux riches*. It is clearly very difficult to grow rich gracefully; but my memories of the war profiteers justify the conviction that there is nothing particularly Jewish or Oriental in the deceitfulness of riches. Moreover, I know more than one Jewish family that has grown rich with dignity and discretion.

It pleases the Jew to thank God that he is not as other men. In the circumstances of his history and of his persecutions by other men, it is perfectly natural that he should find satisfaction in the conviction that he is of different stuff to his persecutors. But the truth is that the Jew is very much like other men, much more than they and he are willing to realize. Such qualities as appear to differentiate the Jews from their fellows are qualities which are theirs conspicuously but which are the marks of the *bourgeois* generally.

If the English are a nation of shopkeepers, they are shopkeepers against their better nature. They have never been content to live in the shop and over the shop. As Mr. Dawson recalls, ever since the sixteenth century the City merchant has loved to found a family and to live in the country. Nevertheless, the English Nonconformists form a society, in many respects similar to the continental *bourgeoisie.* Mr. Dawson says that "their basis of social unity was a religious and not an economic one". I think it was both religious and economic, and in this respect the old-fashioned English Puritan society was similar to the social unity of the Jews.

The Jew's eagerness for education and his persistent interest in the intellectual does not affect the truth of the assertion that he is the *bourgeois par excellence,* for there has always been within the *bourgeois* civilization, not only the personal accumulation of wealth, but the growth of culture and the encouragement of freedom of thought and freedom of expression. And it is this freedom which the Jew has always cherished, that is being destroyed by the anti-*bourgeois* movements of the times.

Here, in England, the Jew is distinguished by his devotion to the family. He has a far acuter sense of family obligation than the average Englishman, and a far greater devotion to family life. It can never, of course, be forgotten that we owe it to the Jew that the family is the basis of Western civilization, and, in the attempt to destroy the family, the Bolshevists are striking at what is one of the many great Jewish gifts to the modern world. But, in his respect for family obligation, the Jew is in no way superior to the French *bourgeois.* Indeed, while the Jew, with his abundant hospitality, warmly welcomes the stranger into the family fold, the middle-class Frenchman surrounds his family with a Chinese wall through which no stranger is permitted to enter. Generally family ties are more definitely respected by the *bourgeoisie* on the Continent than they are in this country, and the Jew has brought with him to England what is not so much a Jewish possession as a possession of middle and western Europe.

The patriarchal idea of the family, which the Jews have always cherished and which Protestantism adopted, differs fundamentally from the family as it is regarded in Catholic civilization, where it is only one of the methods of supplying humanity with the opportunities for a full, satisfying, and noble life. The family is the social base of Catholic civilization, but not its religious basis. To the Jew, and to the Puritan, it is both. The revolt in Europe against Catholic tradition was the prelude to the beginning of industrialism, which would have been impossible if the communal spirit had not been largely lost, and was only made possible by the conviction that it is perfectly right and proper for each family, each little separate unity, to fight for its own hand. So far as this is a Jewish characteristic, it is again a characteristic which he shares with the Protestant *bourgeoisie*.

The Jew has become *bourgeois* by necessity and not by instinct. The commercial eminence of the Scottish people is evidently due to certain inherent national qualities, fostered by the Presbyterian religion. No outside political pressure has compelled the Scots to become the world's supreme traders. But, for centuries, the Jew has been compelled to batten in order to live. And it is a queer fact that Jews and Scotsmen, for all their commercial success, are equally interested in the affairs of the intellect. The history of the Jew in Germany is, indeed, the history of a people eager to escape from the market-place to the schools.

But the *bourgeois* must necessarily be *bourgeois*. If a man's business is to make bargains, he is a fool if he does not use every endeavour to make good bargains, and I do not think that he is much to be blamed if he makes hard bargains. Trading is necessarily haggling. I do not suppose that buying and selling can be either an amusing or an inspiring avocation. It should be—when mankind was sane it always was —good fun to sow and to reap, and to create whether the creation be a chair or a sonnet. The financial reward for such good work is only a small part of the reward, and the men who spend their lives in such work are generally, and quite reasonably, accused by their less fortunate fellows of not knowing " the value of money ". The truth is that they know that money has no value except as a means of securing the pleasant appurtenances of life, among which the smiles of our neighbours are not the least valuable.

To the professional buyer and seller, money becomes something of itself, a possession to be cherished as it were a picture, a garden, or a friend. And to the Jew, as to all the *bourgeoisie* and particularly to the French, there is a thrill in the creation of a bank balance and a consequent respect for the obviously accurate axiom that if a man looks after the pennies the pounds will look after themselves.

There are many pleasanter and ultimately more profitable methods of spending one's days than in looking after either pennies or pounds. But it is muddle-headed to confuse causes with consequences. The Jew has not rejected the better part. He has been, to a large extent, debarred from it. Thanks to the difficulties that he has had to overcome and perhaps to more than an average agility of mind, he has become the *bourgeois par excellence* with all the *bourgeois* virtues and all the *bourgeois* vices well and sometimes over developed.

As a *bourgeois* the Jew is distinguished among his competitors. I have been assured by a number of my commercial acquaintances that the Jew can nearly always be trusted to be true to his bond. He may drive the hardest of hard bargains. To haggle adds zest and perhaps amusement to his trading. But when terms have been accepted, they will be kept.

In two respects the Jew would seem to be untrue to the *bourgeois* type. Unlike the Scotsman, he is much given to gambling, and my experience is that he is often a very poor gambler. But here again the Jew resembles the Frenchman. In Boulogne-sur-Mer, Jean Prudhomme may be seen on any summer evening risking sums on the tables of the Casino that would terrify the respectable citizen of Wimbledon or Golder's Green. Gambling is one of the many methods—perperhaps the most foolish—of escaping from boredom and monotony, and possibly the reason why Jew and Frenchman gamble, while the Scotsman does not is because the Scotsman really enjoys himself behind the counter. But the Scotsman drinks, and that is a very rare Jewish habit. The bottle may be for the Scotsman what a pack of cards is to the Jew—a way of escape.

In one other respect the Jew is unlike both Scot and Frenchman. The Jew loves playing the host. The Jew, rich and poor alike, delights in parties to which Gentile and Jew are welcome. He is certainly nearly always eager for friendship. That is natural when his ancestors have received so little friendship outside their own tribe. I do not believe that, as a rule, he wants to buy smiles with his good food and drink. But he values smiles for all that they may signify. So do the great majority of men, all indeed, except the very few who are detestable. And if the Jew is, as I think he is, more than usually anxious to invite friends and acquaintances to rejoice with him, it is because he wants to make the most of the place in the sun, so recently and so grudgingly ceded to him and still in insistent peril.

The Jew is not, on the whole, distinguished by quickness of perception and understanding. He is, on the other hand, generally sceptical. He is disinclined to take anything on trust. I am told by a distinguished Oxford professor that he always finds Jewish undergraduates less easy to persuade than their fellows, more determined to peep behind the scenes and to look at the works, and less ready to accept any assertion that is not backed by what is to them satisfactory evidence. Here there is a difference between the average Jew and the average Englishman, but there would probably be found to be no such difference between young

Jews and young Frenchmen, the typical European sceptics.

Generally the Jew is distinguished by his capacity for concentration. He is narrow-minded in the sense that his mind is concerned with one thing at a time. He is not easily lured away from the main track to investigate the byways. He has an end steadily in view, and it is this firmness of purpose that is the main cause of his success. If his intention is to make money, his life will probably be a steady progress from comparative poverty to unusual wealth. If, on the other hand, his concern is with scholarship, he will probably be entirely indifferent to money and the things that money can easily and always secure.

The Jew is the *bourgeois*, often the good *bourgeois*, with certain qualities of his own, qualities acquired not in the great days of his people in Palestine, but in the dark days of his people in the ghettoes. His vices, too, are *bourgeois* vices. Criminal statistics prove that everywhere the Jew is rather more law-abiding than his neighbours, and the crimes to which he is addicted are much more often crimes against property than crimes of violence. The Jew in the dock is nearly always a dishonest trader. Long-firm frauds appear to have a particular attraction for the bad Jew; and arson, all over the world, is almost a Jewish monopoly. Arson, as Mr. Polly believed, was an admirable way out of financial difficulties. The Jew has attempted, not without success at times, to make it a means of attaining affluence. I have no sort of notion why the bad Jew prefers one sort of *bourgeois* crime to another, nor do I know why the law-abiding Jew prefers one form of trade to another. I should add that I am convinced that there is no justification for the charge that the Jew controls either the white slave traffic or the illicit drug trade. There are unquestionably Jewish procurers and Jewish 'dope runners', but from the inquiries that I have made it is clear that their numbers are comparatively insignificant.

Mr. Belloc suggests that the Jew loves secrecy. He anglicizes his name, in the hope that if Cohen becomes Curzon the simple Christian fly will be more easily beguiled into the spider's web. There are, of course, predatory Jews, entirely unscrupulous in their methods, and Shylock is still to be found in Jewry. It should be noted that while the money-lenders of Jermyn Street are often Jews, the money-lenders of the industrial towns who lend half-crowns to the harassed mothers of families at four- and five-hundred per cent are never Jews. I do not find any justification for the charge that the Jews generally love to plot in secret. It is always silly for a man to change his name, particularly as he cannot change his features. No one really believes that Cohen-become-Curzon is anything but a Jew; and changing names appears to have been largely given up since the war. As a matter of fact the average Jew is rarely subtle and often unexpectedly ingenuous, much given to the truly Christian practice of giving himself away.

In the Middle Ages circumstances compelled the Jews to huckstering. In the Middle Ages, too, the Church

65

still had the courage to denounce usury, and since medieval kings often wanted to borrow money, the Jew, unaffected by canon law and the wrath of the Church, became the money-lender and the banker. The Jew is still more often a distributor than a manufacturer, though Jewish manufacturing firms are becoming more and more common and important. There may be some moral to be deduced from the fact that the Jew largely controls the cheap clothing trade in every country and is prominent in the tobacco industry, in the sale of jewellery, and in the distribution of vegetables and fruit. I cannot suggest what the moral can be, just as I have never found a satisfactory explanation for the Welsh pre-war monopoly of the London milk trade. These things happen. They are a part of the ever-continuing mystery of life.

To fight for existence in a hostile atmosphere is inevitably to experience a sharpening of the wits. The Jew has always had to beware of the enemy on the right and on the left. Having an experience of commerce, that began many centuries before any European nation became a nation of shopkeepers, he has acquired an hereditary commercial sense, which makes him quick to discover new markets and still to be among the first to appreciate the possibilities of new industries. The cinema industry in America, in England, and in Germany, is controlled by Jewish capitalists, and to a less extent, directed by Jewish artists. The Jews, who reign in Hollywood, are not the most desirable of their race, and in so far as Hollywood is affecting—and it is affecting to an appalling extent —the spiritual outlook and the estimate of values of the more ingenuous of the peoples of a thousand cities, here is one of the few legitimate grounds for anti-Jewish resentment. But the Jewish trek to California was not inspired by any deliberate intention to corrupt the world, but by an early appreciation of the immense financial possibilities of a new industry. Similarly, in a much smaller industry, Jews are largely concerned in the sale of radio accessories, another new trade, the possibilities of which they were among the first to realize.

There is nothing inherent in the Jewish character that impels the Jew to the selling of things rather than to the making of them. Benammi, the author of the extremely interesting "Essays on Jewish Life and Thought", says that in the sixteenth century there were in Berlin 3,200 Jewish traders and 10,000 Jewish craftsmen. In Poland, which in proportion has the largest Jewish population of any country in Europe, the Jews form nearly fifty per cent of all manual workers, and the making of jewellery and watches is almost an exclusively Jewish trade. The Jewish crafts-man is prominent in the precious stone industry in Amsterdam and Antwerp; and in England, not only are the Jews engaged in the manufacture as well as in the selling of cheap clothing, but they are also notably successful as wood-workers.

I pass to another popular conviction. It is said of the Jew that his isolation is self-imposed, that he has resisted and defeated assimilation, that he has deliber-

ately elected to be an alien everywhere. That is partially, but only partially, true. Partly from pride of
race, partly from respect for religion, partly from the
motive of self-protection, the Jew has struggled and
continues to struggle to retain his distinction as a
member of a race apart. In this such men of vastly
different qualities as M. J. Landa, the novelist, who is
Orthodox; Dr. Mattuck, the Liberal rabbi, to whom
Judaism is an inspired religion; and Dr. Weizman, the
Zionist leader, would agree. That, despite the certain
and inevitable mixture of blood, the Jew continues, is,
as I have said, the most obvious miracle of the modern
world. Whether or no the Jews will continue a separate
people I shall discuss in a later chapter. To-day the
separation is cherished, but the Jew himself remains
only as a modified separation. Only rarely does he
wish to remain an alien!

"The Jew", a distinguished man of letters has
written to me, "does not care to work with the Gentile." I showed the statement to the directors of one
of the largest of Jewish-controlled distributing busi-
nesses. "The suggestion is absurd," was their comment. "Our entire success is due to the fact that we
have gained the confidence of non-Jewish manufacturers, who are as glad to work with us as we are to
work with them. And in our house, in considering
employment and promotions we show no preference
for Jews. That would be a suicidal policy. In every
case we are influenced by our estimate of the man, and
the man who is in our judgment best qualified gets the
job, be he Jew or Gentile. The consequence is that

by far the greater number of the leading positions in our firm are held by non-Jews."

The Jew has always been ready to walk with us, talk with us, buy with us, and sell with us. To-day, for the most part, he is delighted to eat with us and drink with us. Some day, perhaps, he will pray with us. To a very large extent it is our fault and not his that he still lives in a sort of modified ghetto. The record of Jews in Western Europe and in America, with the personal experience of non-Jews with intimate contacts with Jews, is a sufficient proof of the unqualified sincerity of the Jewish gesture, "I'd be your friend and have your love."

It is said that the Jew always considers himself first a Jew, then an Englishman, or a German, or a Frenchman. I think that is true of most Jews, though again not of all. But that does not appear to me evil. A man who believes in the Catholic religion and all its implications, must of necessity think of himself first as a member of the Catholic Church, and then as a citizen of his particular nation. Patriotism is a splendid and inspiring possession, but the soul of man cannot be satisfied without a higher, a super-national or at least a supra-national allegiance. But the higher allegiance does not destroy the lower allegiance, and may intensify it. The good Catholic is generally a good Englishman, though that was not believed in Elizabethan England, and was apparently doubted by Charles Kingsley who, Hilaire Belloc suggests, was himself partly Jewish. As with the Catholic, so with the Jew.

F

It is only since the sixteenth century that frontiers have been regarded as the sacrosanct boundaries of the City of God. The scholar, as late as Erasmus, was a nomad, journeying from university to university, indifferent as to whether he was within the territory of the King of France or of the King of England, only conscious that he was dwelling in the land of culture. Similarly the pilgrim made his leisurely and perilous journeys, certain of the aid of the faithful whatever the language that they spoke. The greater allegiance was destroyed when the *Respublica Christiana* was destroyed. It has been preserved for the Jew by his persecutors. The English Jew, possibly with a non-Jewish wife, certainly with many non-Jewish friends, proud of his privileges as a British citizen, and ready enough to be a good and useful citizen, has been recently rudely reminded by Herr Hitler that he is a Jew. His cousins, whom he has never seen, are being harmed. He has heard the call of the blood, that only the mean and despicable can fail to answer.

The persecution of Christians in Bolshevist Russia was every bit as thorough and as brutal as the persecution of Jews in Nazi Germany. The Bolshevist persecution, despite righteous denunciation from Rome and Canterbury, failed to arouse the effective indignation of the nominally Christian nations, and has even found apologists among certain American *soi-disant* Christians. The Nazi persecutions have been much more vigorously denounced both by Jews and non-Jews. Here, says the anti-Semite, is proof of the predominating influence of the Jew. That is not so. It is the proof that race has become a greater spiritual influence than religion. The English Jew is vitally concerned by the troubles of the German Jew. The English Christian cared little for the troubles of the Russian Christian.

There is much to be said for the ideal "one nation, one religion". It was the ideal of Catherine de Medici, of Elizabeth, and of Louis XIV. It is necessary for the success of both Bolshevism and Fascism. But in a democratic state, the practice of the Jewish religion need not separate a man from his fellows any more than the practice of one or other of the countless varieties of Protestant Christianity, particularly as, in their fundamentals, there is little difference between Liberal Judaism and the Unitarianism which has, in the last few years, largely permeated certain of the Protestant sects.

With all this, it would be absurd to suggest that there is no sort of separatism. Of course there is. Perhaps because of the centuries of persecution, perhaps because of his feeling that he is still regarded with a certain suspicion, perhaps because of his proper pride in his race, the Jew, often though by no means always, feels himself a foreigner, a naturalized foreigner, very content to be a citizen of this or that country, obedient to its laws, eager for its service, generous in friendship with his fellow citizens, but none the less a foreigner. To my surprise this was emphasized to me by a Jew, whom I have always regarded as a particularly attractive member of the class of Englishmen among whom he was born and whose virtues and prejudices he obviously shares. "I always feel," he said, "the grati-

tude of the foreigner for the friendship and the kindness
that I receive every day of my life." My friend's family
has been settled in England for generations. Its members have been distinguished in commerce, in public
affairs, and in the Army. He himself is a man of unusual sensibility. Perhaps that is why he professes
that he is not quite at home in the only home that he
has.

One of the most perplexing sides of the Jewish puzzle
is that Jews fundamentally disagree in their reactions to
a Gentile society. I have quoted what one of my friends
has told me. Another, also a man of character and distinction, but only the second generation of his family
in this country, born and educated in England but far
less English in mind and nature than my first friend,
protested that he has never felt himself a foreigner here.
He would describe himself as an English Jew. His sons
may perhaps describe themselves as Jewish Englishmen.

The suggestion that a Jew must remain an alien can
have no other justification except the grotesque belief
that modern nations consist of individuals of one racial
stock. This theory is to-day most popular in Germany
where there is much talk of Nordic blood and pan-
Aryan descent, and nowhere is the talk more absurd for
there is certainly a large strain of Slav blood in the
Prussians, and as Dean Inge, who has himself flirted
with the Nordic absurdity, has unkindly pointed out
" the typical German skull is predominantly Alpine ".
The English are mainly Teuton, in their descent, but
Teuton modified by the Celt, and who can say what

eccentric ancestry we may owe to the Roman legions, recruited in " the regions beyond Jordan ". The ' pure blood ' fanatic has all the facts against him.

In modern history, too, the alien born or the alien descended has often become eminent among the nationals of his adopted country. On every Primrose Day, the squires from the shires and the spinsters from the spas still pay their tribute to Benjamin Disraeli as the noble champion of blue-blooded Toryism. Joseph Conrad, the Pole, became one of the masters of English fiction, as the Greek Moréas was one of the most gifted of French poets of his time. And who is more English than Mr. Hilaire Belloc, the son of a French father? Who has sung more charmingly of the joy and beauty of the English countryside? Who was ever more properly jealous for England's honour? But Mr. Belloc, who has wiped out a frontier for himself, insists that the Jew can never become anything but just a Jew.

He says (p.73): " Jews are often accused of cowardice, avarice and treason. You examine their actions and you find innumerable instances of the highest courage, the greatest generosity and the most devoted loyalty." No one will question that this is true. But when Mr. Belloc adds that the courage, generosity and loyalty are " of a Jewish kind, directed to Jewish ends and stamped with a highly distinctive Jewish mark ", he is writing with unreasonable prejudice. I have no sort of idea of what can be the difference between Jewish courage and non-Jewish courage. But the generosity of Jews, not only to their fellow-Jews, but in all their contacts with the society of which they form a part, is

73

notorious. And in using the word generosity I am not merely thinking of a philanthropy exhibited in charitable contributions, but generosity in judgment and a really unusual capacity for sympathy and understanding. It is certainly not the fact that Jews are merely loyal to their own traditions and to their own community. They are loyal nationals in the countries in which they live, though perhaps not prone to the exaggerated jingoism that makes patriotism ridiculous. They are loyal to their friends, and loyal to their word and their bond. All this is confirmed by a cloud of Christian witnesses.

" Directed to Jewish ends and stamped with a highly distinctive Jewish mark " ! To what " Jewish end " are Sir Herbert Samuel's British politics directed ? What is the peculiar Jewish mark in Siegfried Sassoon's pacifist poetry ? Were the Jewish soldiers in all the armies during the war fighting for Jewish ends ? When Preuss drew up the Weimar Constitution was the claim that he was endeavouring to create a progressive German democracy, that might again acquire the best that had been lost in the war, a mere pretence ?—and is Hitler right in his charge that the one object of Preuss and his colleagues was to deliver Germany into the hands of the Jews ? Was Walther Rathenau really thinking of a new Judæa and not of a new Europe when he wrote *In Days to Come*? Such questions are sufficient to show that Mr. Belloc's charge is mere lawyer's rhetoric.

It is of course obvious that, when the Jew was forced to emigrate from the Rhine valley to Poland, he was not moved by a yearning to become a patriotic Pole and faithfully to serve Casimir the Great. It is equally obvious that when, centuries later, he migrated from Poland and Galicia, to London, and New York, he was not journeying with the high ambition of ranging himself with Shakespeare and Nelson, or with Washington and Lincoln. Mr. Belloc is right. The nomad, against his will, was seeking " safety first ". Mr. Belloc writes (pp. 26, 27): " What the Jew wanted was not the proud privilege of being called an Englishman, a Frenchman, an Italian, or a Dutchman. To this he was completely indifferent (for his pride lay in being a Jew, his loyalty was to his own, and what is more, he might at any moment fold up his tent and go off to another country for good). What the Jew wanted was not the feeling that he was just like the others—that would have been odious to him—what he wanted was *security*; it is what every human being craves for, and what he of all men most lacked; the power to feel safe in the place where one happens to be."

Mr. Belloc admits that in his endeavour to find security the Jew was only sharing a universal human craving. But in the passage I have quoted there are two suggestions that are open to criticism. The first is that the Jew never regards himself as a settler, that his instinct is always to move on. There is nothing in his history to prove this assumption. The Jew had been in the Rhine Valley for centuries before the Black Death when he was charged with having poisoned the wells, and with thus having brought the pestilence on the people, and was compelled to move eastward. It was the Tsarist pogroms that impelled the Jew to emigrate to America and England. It is persecution to-day in Germany that is causing the Jew to cross the frontiers into Holland, Belgium, and France; and a considerable proportion of the ' nomads ', reasonably, as Mr. Belloc would agree, seeking security, belong to families that have been in Germany for four and five hundred years.

The second suggestion that, having sought and found security, the Jew is indifferent to the privileges and responsibilities of the citizenship that he has acquired is, as I have already argued, quite untrue.

The contention would seem to be that the Jew is still an Asiatic sojourner in Europe and America, as different in essentials from the Briton, the German, the Frenchman, or the citizen of the United States, as the Persian, the Indian, or the Japanese. To accept this contention is to profess to be able to determine the definitely Asiatic qualities, whatever they may be, possessed to-day by Sir Herbert Samuel and, say, by my friend S. L. Bensusan, the charming country writer; by Bruno Walther, and Emil Ludwig, and Einstein; by Jesse Strauss, the American Ambassador in Paris; and Walter Lippmann, the American philosopher. Can any reasonable person really believe that Bagdad is the spiritual home of these men? What Asiatic quality is there in the poetry of Heine, the music of Mendelssohn, Meyerbeer and Saint-Saëns; the fiction of Disraeli or, if you will Gilbert Frankau, the philosophy of Spinoza, or the political idealism of Walther Rathenau? The Jew may be a nuisance, he may be a peril, he may be a problem. But he is at least a European nuisance, a European peril and a European problem.

THE QUALITIES OF THE JEW

The Jew has been in Europe for over a thousand years. The late Lucien Wolf says in his article on anti-Semiticism in the *Encyclopædia Britannica*:

> In the ghetto the pastoral Semite, who had been made a wanderer by the destruction of his nationality, was steadily trained through centuries, to become an urban European, with all the parasitic activities of urban economics. . . . Thus the Jew who emerged from the ghetto was no longer a Palestinian Semite, but an essentially modern European, who differed from his Christian fellow-countrymen only in the circumstances that his religion was of the older Semitic form, and that his physical type had become sharply defined through a slightly more rigid exclusiveness in the matter of marriages than that practised by Protestants and Roman Catholics.

"His physical type has become sharply defined", but it should be remembered that, while in England the fact that a man is a Jew is generally, though not always, made clear by his features, there is physiognominally little difference between the Jew and the Southern Italian, or even the southern Frenchman, and far less between the Jew and the Armenian. A middle-aged Italian woman from Calabria would certainly be taken for a Jewess by nine out of ten passers-by if she were taken for a walk in Regent Street.

In this connexion it is interesting to note how fundamentally the Jew is affected by his environment, in this being as other men. Yiddish, the *lingua franca* of the Jew, is a bastard European language written in Hebrew script. Its basis is Middle German, and the Jews took the language with them when they went to Poland. In the course of the ages many Polish words have been added to it, so that to-day the Yiddish of Warsaw is very different from the Yiddish of Frankfort, and the Yiddish of Whitechapel and the Yiddish of the Bowery have their definite English and American additions.

Similarly the mentality of the various European nations is evident at Zionist conferences. The Western Jew has the caution that is one of the results (perhaps one of the evil results) of experience of democratic government. The Eastern Jew, seeing the light for the first time after centuries of darkness, is impatient of compromise and scornful of half measures. I am told, too, that in any large international assembly of Jews, it is quite easy to pick out the various nationals from their appearance before a word has been spoken.

The modern world—by which I mean modern Europe and America—belongs to the Jew as it belongs to the rest of us. He has made his contribution to its development and culture. If he is unaffected by its prevailing religion, so are the majority of his non-Jewish compatriots. If in some respects he is peculiar, in many more he is even as you and I.

Separatism has been vastly exaggerated. But I do not say that it does not exist. The Jewish community very much resembles the Quakers, who adhere to a tradition many centuries younger than the Jewish tradition, and who, like the Jews, pay to-day a certain homage to a religion the peculiar tenets of which most of them have abandoned. There is a certain habit of mind that generally characterizes the Quaker, and there is a certain habit of mind that generally characterizes the Jews, but which in neither case creates any real spiritual barrier between them and " us others ".

The most obvious differences between Jews and non-Jews is neither intellectual nor spiritual, but temperamental. As a result of centuries of persecution, the possession of Jewish blood carries with it a common, indeed almost universal, tendency to hysteria. Nine out of ten Jews are ' nervy '. Most of the men who during the war served at the front while they were boys, are jumpy, easily excited, inclined to exaggeration. Some of them are definitely and obviously ill-balanced. Jewish ' nerviness ' has a similar origin. The majority of Jews in this country are the descendants, probably in the third generation, of men who survived a series of pogroms, who saw their fathers and mothers killed in cold blood, and who shivered in childish horror of violence and death. Add to this that, when frontiers were passed and personal security attained, life was lived in an atmosphere of suspicion, dislike and resentment; the child bullied, and derided as a ' sheeny ' and a ' dirty Jew-boy '; the success of youth resented and disparaged, every gesture of friendship misrepresented, always the suggestion, often openly expressed, that a Jew's room is better than his company.

The Jew has " grown familiar with disfavour, grown familiar of the savour of the bread by which men die ". What is the result? The paradoxical possession of both a superiority and an inferiority complex, the proud hugging of a great tradition which makes contemptible the petty rudeness of men of a race that the Almighty could never conceivably have chosen, and at the same time the expectation of insult and slights even where they are most unlikely. And this inheritance of the fear of persecution has had its inevitable effect on the Jewish nerves. In his *Jewish Life in Modern Times*, (p. 109), Israel Cohen says:

> The liability of the Jews to nervous diseases is a subject of peculiar and pathetic interest. Distinguished by the superiority of their nervous over their muscular system, they are more prone to mental affections than other people in whom the nervous system is relatively less highly developed. According to various authorities the frequency of mental diseases among Jews is from four to five times higher than among non-Jews. It is chiefly nervous diseases of a functional order, however, to which they are subject, particularly neurasthenia and hysteria, the latter being found among males to a notable degree.

The tendency to hysteria is something of a peculiarity in England, even though the boast that the English are a stolid self-controlled people is not, I believe, justified by fact. Mr. Shaw is perfectly right in his assertion, in the preface to *John Bull's Other Island*, that the English are essentially romantic. But romanticism and even sentimentality are not neurotic. Because he is romantic the Englishman laughs at misfortune and always hopes for the best. When the Jew weeps, the non-Jew in England will often laugh, but his heart is equally heavy, and he is merely engaged in the romantic endeavour to laugh it off. But the Jew knows that the thing that matters can never be laughed off. He is the heir of the sorrow of the ages. "It might be worse," is the common English attitude to calamity and misfortune. " The worst is almost certain to happen " is the common anticipation of the Jew.

I have discussed this particular side of the Jewish character with two practising physicians, one of them with many years' experience in the East End, the other with a large practice in Kensington. They both agree that if a Jew has a stomach-ache, he almost invariably expects an early death, and if one of his children is a little sick, he is in a fever of exaggerated apprehension. He will rush to the surgery or the consulting-room, forgetting the courtesy due to other patients—and normally the Jew does not lack courtesy —and will insist on immediate attention. This insistence is the result of ' nerves ' and of deep family affection.

Similarly in the East End the death of a child is the occasion of shrill and persistent lamentation—here custom and ritual stimulating hysteria—that is in grim contrast to the philosophic, almost sullen resignation of the Gentile neighbours. But the Jew generally grows into the atmosphere in which he lives and, taking on the quality of the people around him, he begins to acquire self-control. He still feels acutely. But he learns to hold himself in hand. The Jew wails at the Wall in Jerusalem. He does not wail in the squares of Mayfair. He has acquired "the stiff upper lip ".

The sub-conscious memory of persecution is one of the reasons for Jewish family affection. The race must be carried on. The " young child " was always in danger. The Jews still marry young and, until recent years, they have generally had considerable families. The increasing knowledge of the methods of birth prevention is now affecting the Jew as well as the non-Jew, and with security assured there is no longer the common acceptance that domestic happiness is dependent on accepting the admonition of the Psalmist: "Thy wife shall be as a fruitful vine in the innermost parts of thy house: thy children like olive plants about thy table." Family feeling, however, continues, even though the families are smaller, and the traditional belief remains that Jewish children are the peculiar gifts of God to the world.

This makes the attitude of Jewish parents to their children much softer and more tolerant than it is in non-Jewish families. Frankly, it is my experience that the majority of Jewish children are completely spoiled and are often extremely difficult to endure; and my doctor friends, from whom I have already quoted, are emphatic in their agreement. But the capacity of the Jew to adapt himself to environment makes the boy and girl, who are almost intolerable in the family circle, courteous and disciplined at school, and at adolescence as pleasant as the average of the young people around them. It is the genius of the Jew to retain all that is ennobling in tradition, and to shed most of its evil consequences.

This, then, is my answer to the question: What is the Jew? I have tried, quite dispassionately, to examine his qualities. I find that, considering his history, the differences between him and his fellows are amazingly few and generally unessential. He has been hated, but he has never shown any great capacity for hatred. He has been persecuted but, even to the surprise of his persecutors, he has rarely tried to persecute. He has been condemned to humiliation in this world and damnation in the world to come, and he has replied with assurance: " The Good Men of the Gentile races will inherit the World to Come."

CHAPTER 3

DOES THE JEW MATTER?

THERE are approximately between fifteen and sixteen
million Jews in the world to-day. The statistics have
been very carefully compiled by Mr. Israel Cohen,
who, however, admits that they are of necessity
approximate. "Only in a comparatively few countries
does the government census take note of differences
of religion and ethnical nationality, so that in the case
of other countries we have to content ourselves with
estimates made either by the government authorities
or the local Jewish communities." It is clear that,
when the number of Jews is taken as the number of
members of the congregations, the estimate will be
too low, although it is to be remembered that many
Jews who do not practise the Jewish religion or do
not even attend synagogue on the Day of Atonement,
remain members of some congregation, from respect
for tradition or to ensure burial in a Jewish cemetery.
It has been suggested to me that the generally accepted
figure of 600,000 as the Jewish population of Germany
represents the equivalent of communicants of the
Christian Church, and that the actual number of Jews
in Germany, including those not practising the Jewish
religion with the nominal and sincere converts to

84

Christianity, is very much larger. Mr. Bernays puts the number at a million and a half. If the Nazi theory that every one with twenty-five per cent Jewish blood is a Jew, be accepted, it is far more than that. Before the war there were many social and professional reasons why a German Jew should become Christian, but those reasons were destroyed by the Weimar Constitution, and Colonel Waley Cohen thinks that the number of German-Jewish Christians to-day is fewer than one per thousand.

I have gone carefully through the names of distinguished English Jews in the *Jewish Year Book*, and I have found many notable omissions. There are, for example, a certain number of Jewish Christians in England, among them three well-known priests of the English Church, an Anglican Lord Justice, and a Roman Catholic humorist. None of their names is in the *Year Book* list, which also bans Jews like Gilbert Frankau who I do not think will be hurt if I call him a convinced assimilationist. I think, therefore, that Mr. Cohen's estimate in the 1929 edition of his book *Jewish Life in Modern Times* of 15,218,734 as the world's Jewish population is probably an understatement, and that the figure should be probably rather more than 16,000,000.

Taking the figure as 16,000,000, approximately 10,000,000 Jews live in Europe, approximately 5,000,000 in America, and 1,000,000 in the rest of the world. In Europe it is generally estimated that there are 3,000,000 Jews in Poland, some 2,750,000 in Russia, 1,000,000 in Rumania, 600,000 in Germany,

500,000 in Hungary, 300,000 in Great Britain and Ireland—Colonel Waley Cohen puts the number at 220,000—200,000 in France, and 50,000 in Italy. In most cases I have slightly added to Mr. Israel Cohen's figures. The Jewish percentage of the various populations is ten in Poland, six in Hungary, two in Holland, four in Austria, one in Germany, three in Russia, three-quarters of one in Great Britain, and half of one in France. The percentage is high in the Balkan States of Lithuania and Latvia. Considerably more than four-fifths of the Jews in America live in the United States, and half of them in the three cities of New York, Chicago, and Philadelphia. Jews are thirty per cent of the total population in New York, where there are more than five times the total Jewish population of Great Britain and Ireland. Jews are more than forty-four per cent of the population of Odessa, thirty-five per cent of the population of Lemberg, thirty-four per cent of the population of Warsaw, over ten per cent of the population of Chicago and Amsterdam, and only about three per cent of the population of London.

The most amazing fact about Jewish statistics is that the Jewish population is said to have increased by some four hundred per cent in the past hundred years, and this despite the persecutions and the forced migrations.

Here then is a people, in all considerably fewer than the population of Rumania, scattered all over the world, bound together by the same traditions, and, to an extent, by the same faith. But that is all. Perhaps the majority of Jews have some knowledge of Hebrew as a liturgical language, as the Roman Catholics have some knowledge of Latin. A certain number, but a definite minority, can speak and read Hebrew. The majority speak Yiddish, but Yiddish varies with the cities. And a considerable percentage speak only the language of the country in which they live, and where are all their material interests. What in common have the 300,000 Jews in Philadelphia and the 50,000 in Bagdad—the 100,000 in Buenos Ayres and the 70,000 in Minsk?

It is asserted in *The International Jew*, a crude enough publication, I admit, but widely read and accepted: " Judaism is the most closely organised power on earth, even more than the British Empire. It forms a State whose citizens are unconditionally loyal wherever they may be and whether rich or poor. ' All Judaism ' is the only State that exercises world government.'' As a matter of fact there is no such thing as ' All Judaism '. ' International Jewry ' is a phrase. And it is only on rare occasions and for very short periods that the Jews of the world ever act together.

Consider the current anti-Semitic charge that the Jews are responsible for the world chaos, secretly prepared by the Elders of Zion, in order that the Jew may wax rich while the Christian grows more harassed and lean. The world's misfortunes are the heritage of the war. It is a Marxian maxim that all wars have an economic origin. That is a fallacy. Wars are the result of sentiment, of dynastic or national am-

bitions and fears, or of political considerations of
which the fear of internal revolution is the most
frequent. Sir Norman Angell, a man gifted with a
large measure of common sense, and realizing, as few
other men realized, that war would cost the victor
quite as much as it cost the vanquished, boldly declared in 1912 that there would never be another great
European war. But Sir Norman Angell supposed that
national policies are affected by common sense. He
did not understand the unchallengable authority of
folly in the Chancellories. There is now abundant
evidence to justify the statement that Europe was led
to disaster in 1914 by short-visioned, ill-informed *soi-
disant* statesmen, few of them actually wanting war,
but without the smallest notion of what a modern war
must be; some of them dreading war, but too bewildered and too timorous to take any effective step
to prevent it. The Jews, as a body, were as much
responsible for the war as the Abyssinians, though
there may have been sections of Jews, as there were
sections of Gentiles, who benefited by the war.

There is evidence that certain well-informed persons,
with an acute appreciation of European conditions,
believed that war would break out in 1914. In a
pamphlet, *The Secret International Armament Firms
at Work*, it is stated that "the files at Somerset
House show there was a feverish anxiety to deal in
armament shares in the summer of 1914". This does
not imply that those well-informed persons had deliberately plotted, but only that they had wit enough
to foresee the result of folly in high places. There may

have been Jews among them, but they were certainly not all or mainly Jews. Indeed if the Jews generally had foreseen war they would surely have had some thought for their German co-religionists, who stood to lose their all from war.

The war broke out, and a number of people did very well out of it. Jewish firms in England made large war profits out of clothing and oilskins, and Jewish firms in America had their share of the flood of war profits that entered that country. But that is beside the point. It would be ridiculous to suggest that the war-profiteer had foresight enough or influence enough to have prepared for years to set the nations by the ears that his bank balance might become swollen. Profits came to the profiteer as manna from Heaven. It is, however, worth noting as an example that nothing is too absurd to be believed, that in a pamphlet published in Munich in 1919 Germany's downfall was ascribed to a plot between Jewry and the British people, who are, according to the British Israelite theory, the Lost Tribes!

After the war, the Treaty! There is common agreement that the terms of the Peace Treaty are largely responsible for the present confusion. " Hitler ", it is said, " was born at Versailles." Jews certainly had nothing to do with the treaties, those masterpieces of ignorance, prejudice, and revenge. There was no Jew among the plenipotentiaries in Paris, though I remember stories of mysterious secret interviews at the Hotel Crillon between an American and a German banker after the German delegation had come to Versailles. Whatever the Berlin banker may have said to his cousin from New York can have had little good effect from his point of view, because it is notorious that German bankers and financiers, Jew and Gentile alike, have suffered immense losses from the war, while the Jews are now faced with ruin from political and financial developments for which international bankers are largely responsible.

A real world settlement might have been effected if Woodrow Wilson had not been repudiated by the American people, and if America had been, from the beginning, a member of the League of Nations. The action of America was dictated by the narrow and ill-informed anti-European feeling of the Middle-West, and there is no reason whatever to suppose that it was jerrymandered for some mysterious reason by New York Jewish financiers.

The history of the post-war years is a crazy phantasm, the heyday of false prophets, when everything foretold has not come to pass and only the unexpected has happened. The plain man has ceased to try and understand the respective merits of deflation and inflation, and whether it is more advantageous to be off than to be on the gold standard. He has lost all faith in experts. He is over-taxed. Everything costs him more. He must perforce be content to muddle along. He leaves Mr. J. M. Keynes and his friends to argue, being quite certain that none of them has the smallest idea of what the morrow will bring forth.

DOES THE JEW MATTER?

The financiers have been busy. Week after week Mr. Montagu Norman has made mysterious voyages, and there are innumerable indications of international working agreements as there are innumerable indications that the interests of the financiers and of the manufacturers and traders and, ultimately, of the workers, whom they employ, are generally opposed. Writing of the condition of affairs in Germany in 1930 in their pamphlet "The Crisis", Ernest Bevin and G. D. H. Cole say:

"A German collapse would have involved disastrous consequences for the financiers of New York and London; and both the United States and Great Britain hastened to the rescue. Mr. Hoover put forward his plan for a moratorium on War Debts and Reparations, in order to afford a breathing-space; and the British and other bankers made them to tide over the emergency. By these means, German default and probably German revolution as well were prevented for the moment. But nothing was done to cure the trouble, or to stop its recurrence as soon as the effect of the emergency measures had worn off."

Here is international finance, at which Socialists are continually girding, in action. To the outsider the international financiers seem singularly stupid and incompetent people. Their "extended special loans" have been of precious little good to Germany or to their own interests. They may have staved off a Communist revolution, but they have not prevented the Nazi revolution, which will apparently involve the same "disastrous consequences for the financiers of

New York and London ". How far are these financiers, whose influences in world affairs is either
mischievous, ineffective, or both, Jewish? I turn to
Ernest Franklin, a partner in the firm of Samuel
Montagu & Co., for an answer. In an interesting
paper *The International Financial Jew*, Franklin says
that since the war there has been " a remarkable
decline in the relative positions of Jews and Gentiles in
international finance ". Foreign exchange business has
increased, and many banks that did not formerly deal
in foreign exchanges have become active in that
direction. Franklin adds: " So far as I know, not
one of these firms or banks is managed by Jews, and
no Jewish house has, since the war, established
branches abroad, in the way so many of the English
Joint Stock Banks have done." To this statement I
may add the following quotation from a letter from a
well-known London financial journalist, who is not a
Jew, and who says: " In London, at least, Jews are
playing a far less prominent part than before the war.
If you look through the list of men in key positions in
the City of London, such as the Governor of the Bank
of England, the Five Bank chairmen, the principal
men in the great accepting-houses, you will find that
the Jews are in a small minority. Even Rothschilds is
not the power that it used to be."

Franklin says that since the war the English joint-
stock banks have added to the ramifications of their
business which now includes " foreign exchange,
various loan issues, acceptances, credits both to
governments and to merchants, and other important

international ramifications ". And he adds that not one of these banks has a Jewish manager, and scarcely one a Jewish director. Franklin goes on:

Take the great Eastern banks that finance the trade of the Indian Empire and practically monopolise that of the Chinese Republic, these banks are managed exclusively by non-Jews, generally by Scotsmen. It is the same with the British banks working in Australia, South Africa, and Canada, and with the British banks trading with South America. . . . The foreign exchange business which forty years ago was practically monoplised in this country by Jews, is now almost entirely out of their hands, only one or two Jewish firms take anything like the leading position in that market. The discounting of commercial and high class finance paper is almost exclusively in non-Jewish hands. . . . Even on the Stock Exchange, where Jews held until quite recent times a position out of all proportion to their number, the relative positions of Jew and non-Jew have been changing year by year until to-day the Jewish influence is very small and Gentile firms, with, of course, a certain number of exceptions, monopolise the highest class and most profitable business of the House.

This statement has been confirmed for me by more than one well-informed non-Jewish financial journalist. Franklin is of course only speaking of London, which is still the most important financial centre in the world. But what he says of London is, I believe, true of Paris, and largely true of New York. It was not true of Germany, before the Hitler revolution, where such firms as the Warburgs were the greatest private banking firms with international relations.

It is difficult to find any evidence that, as the

93

Socialists believe, financiers regularly act together for some well-defined and selfish end, and I am persuaded that Mr. Belloc's belief that Jewish bankers, small enough in number to sit at one dinner table, control international finance, is quite fantastic.

It is clear, indeed, that such power as the Jewish financier possessed has been very largely destroyed. Rothschilds has by common consent nothing like the importance that it used to have, and the Jewish bankers in Germany had their prosperity largely affected by the war and have now been practically destroyed by the Hitler revolution. Jewry, says the author of *The International Jew*, "rules as a super-nation over the nations, rules by the power of gold, and plays nation against nation for his own purposes, remaining himself discreetly in the background". Every one of these statements is untrue.

But suppose that there was any element of truth in any one of them, what a short-sighted fool the Jew must be, since war and the aftermath of war have cost his people so dearly!

There is one particular incident in recent history to which I must refer. The fall of the Labour Government in 1929 was due to the refusal of the New York bankers to lend Great Britain sufficient money to prevent most of the things that have happened since, without a pledge from the Cabinet to cut down expenditure on social services. Was this attempt of foreign financiers to interfere with the affairs of this country of Jewish contrivance? It was most certainly not. So far as Great Britain is concerned, New York finance is J. P. Morgan, and all the Jewish financiers in America, counted together, have nothing like the influence of this Napoleon of finance.

In so far then as international finance has influenced world affairs during the past twenty years, generally making confusion worse confounded, the Jew has been concerned, when he has been concerned at all, only as an occasional junior partner. There has been no Jewish international financial combine attempting to affect world affairs to secure definite and particularist Jewish advantage. I doubt whether the money kings of this world have the supreme influence with which they are often credited. They may possibly plan policies and weave plots, but, over and over again, they are engulfed by waves of popular sentiment and hysteria. But, be that as it may, the Jews are not enthroned in the seats of the mighty, though a handful of them may have their places on the steps of the throne. It is not wily Jewish millionaires who are responsible for the ills of this generation, but nationalistic fears, suspicions and jealousies, which a bankrupt European statesmanship is utterly unable to allay, and for which the Jew is now paying with the rest of us.

It would, of course, be ridiculous to deny that 'rings' exist, and to deny that their existence is a menace to the public weal. There is, indeed, one International which is among the greatest existing menaces to the peace and happiness of mankind. I am one of those persons who believe in the existence of the devil, and never, as it seems to me, has the devil been so busy and so successful as in the years since the war. The nations have been persistently endeavouring to arrive at agreements that will save them from mutual destruction. They meet together with sincere goodwill. They talk and they talk, and that is all. Effective action is prevented by some malign influence. The devil is abroad! To discover his instrument in the war against peace it is only necessary to determine to whom war is a pleasant and profitable business, and these people are obviously the makers of armaments, who are allied together in a powerful international federation, and who are assured of vast profits when men begin to kill one another on a wholesale scale.

In England the principal armament firm is Vickers-Armstrong, an amalgamation of a number of great manufacturing concerns, with works all over the country and with a capital of many millions of pounds. In France is the similarly great firm of Schneider Creusot, the directors of which own newspapers, control banks, and are allied with the Skoda armament works in Czecho-Slovakia. It is said that during the past few years the Schneider firm has delivered armaments to Mexico, Yugo-Slavia, Japan, Rumania, Turkey, Bulgaria, Montenegro, Russia, Argentina, Spain, and Italy. The Skoda Company made handsome contributions to the Hitler election campaign, and there is every reason to believe that the international armament ring carries on a persistent and evil anti-pacifist campaign through newspapers and through politicians, and that it is partly due to its tireless activity that the Disarmament Conference in Geneva has proved so bitter a disappointment.

Who are the men behind this secret international? The most important figure is Sir Basil Zaharoff—the friend of Venizelos and Lloyd George—the mystery man of Europe, a Greek by birth, an English knight, the possessor of high French decorations; the man who, during the war, was insistent that there should be " a fight to a finish ". If Sir Basil were a Jew, the anti-Semites would have a case indeed, but, fortunately, he is not.

It is almost certain that the Schneider family is of Alsatian-Jewish origin, and there are, of course, many Jewish holders of shares in the armament companies, though I am told by members of the London Stock Exchange that Jews generally are not particularly interested in such investments.

One concern, and in some respects the most important, was, however, founded by a Jew and is still, to an extent, directed by Jews. I am referring to the Imperial Chemical Industries, which has (so it is said) almost a monopoly for the supply of poison-gas and explosives, and which has a capital of over £70,000,000. The I.C.I. was the creation of the late Lord Melchett; Lord Reading is the president, and the present Lord Melchett is one of the directors, his father, however, having been succeeded in the chairmanship by Sir Harry MacGowan. There are some hundred-thousand shareholders in the I.C.I., and only a comparatively small number of the shares are held by Jews. Among, therefore, the moneyed minority that stands to make money out of death and destruction, there are no more Jews than there are in any other commercial concern, and, if the Schneiders are disregarded, there is hardly a Jew in any of the key positions. The chairman of the I.C.I. is Sir Harry MacGowan; the chairman of Vickers-Armstrong is Sir Herbert Lawrence; and the man with the most widely distributed interest in the armament industry is Sir Basil Zaharoff.

Jews are largely concerned with the second great international combine, the oil combine, which, in its ramifications, affects politics and may be the instrument of widespread mischief in its search for profits. Now that oil has taken the place of coal for the running of warships, Great Britain must of necessity ensure an adequate supply, which means in effect the political control of certain oil-fields. Here then is the always dangerous alliance of national and commercial interests, and I imagine that there may be certain justification for the Bolshevist charge that the development of the Soviet oil-fields is constantly made difficult by the considered opposition of Western capitalists and governments. Shell-Mex is an important member of the oil combine, and Shell-Mex was founded by Lord Bearsted, and its control remains in the hands of the Samuel family. But the great figure in the oil world is not a Jew, but Sir Henry Deterding, who is a Dutch Lutheran, while the great Standard Oil Trust of America, the typical creation of modern capitalism, is the child of that ancient Baptist, John D. Rockefeller.

These two great commercial alliances, therefore,

cannot properly be described as predominantly Jewish. Their success and their failure would affect a certain number of Jews, but they would affect a far larger number of Christians, and the direction of their policy is, only to a comparatively small extent, in Jewish hands.

The metal trade is, of course, directly connected with the manufacture of armaments, and here too the Jew is considerably concerned. Mr. Belloc goes so far as to say that the Jews control the supply of lead, nickel, and mercury, and I am told that the Guggenheims of New York have an absolute control of the American copper market, and that they can jerry-mander the supply of the metal and the prices of stock for their own advantage and to the disadvantage of the users of the metal. This is a case of Jewish commercial activity that may be definitely anti-social. But the Guggenheims are concerned with the fortunes of the Guggenheims, and not with the establishment of a Jewish domination of industry as a whole or, indeed, of this one particular industry. They have quite reasonably earned the dislike of persons who have lost their fortunes on account of Guggenheim plottings. But this one example, not by any means an isolated example, but one of a comparative few, set against the other facts which I have enumerated, cannot be taken as any sort of proof that the Jews are a peril or that they are combined in a campaign of destruction.

Indeed, a cursory study of the Jew in the modern commercial world shows that his interest is in construction, first, naturally, for his own benefit, but ultimately for the benefit of the society to which he belongs. It is, for example, a matter of common agreement that the first essential, if industrial prosperity is to be recovered, is to stimulate consumption. It is quite obvious that the talk of over-production is wicked nonsense so long as any one single individual lacks the necessities of a decent life. In the world to-day the barns and the warehouses are filled to overflowing, while the people, who badly need their contents, are unable to buy. This is not the place to discuss the many sides of the problem of stimulating consumption, but it is evidently necessary to decrease the cost of production by securing for the manufacturer a steady market which will enable him to modernize machinery, to cut down his overhead charges, to decrease the cost of distribution by the elimination, so far as possible, of the middleman, and thus to bring the consumer closer to the producer. This is being done by the multiple stores, and in this new form of distribution, both in this country, in America, in Germany, and in France, the Jew is largely concerned, though the trade is by no means a Jewish monopoly, and the most important of the chain stores in England and America are not Jewish at all.

There is a sound economic theory behind the direction of this sort of business. By the reduction of prices, the real value of wages is enhanced, while at the same time employment is provided and factory profits are assured. It is, therefore, not too much to say that, so far as he is concerned with the cheapening of distribution, the Jew is co-operating in an enterprise of general social advantage, and that he is proving himself a useful member of the community, even though his usefulness may be accompanied by considerable advantage to himself and his family.

The Jewish money-lender is a public pest. The Jewish monopolist may be a public danger, but the Jewish trader is generally honest and always enterprising and, sometimes, as I have said, of outstanding value. But with all this, in the world of trade, he does not matter any more than in the narrower world of finance. He is there, one among many, and ultimately his interests are not the interests of Jews, but the interests of that particular section of society, the modern *bourgeoisie*, with which he is identified.

One more assertion has to be examined. It is asserted by his critics that the Jew controls the world's Press and can thus influence public opinion and compel the Christian to dance to the Jewish pipe. What are the facts? In England there is not one single Jewish-owned newspaper with the exception of the *Sunday Referee*, which can hardly be regarded as the possessor of any great influence. Ralph Blumenfeld is the one editor of outstanding distinction within my experience who is a Jew by birth. There are a number of talented Jewish-English journalists, some of them critics of the arts, one or two writers on public affairs, a handful in less distinguished positions. It is really banal to suggest that the popular English Press is to any extent directed or controlled by Jews. It might be less vulgar if it were. J. S. Elias, the managing director of Odhams, is a Jew, but the agreement under which Messrs. Odhams became part-proprietors of the *Daily Herald* entirely prevents the directors of Odhams from changing the political policy of that newspaper.

The suggestion that the Jews control the Press is difficult to answer, because any newspaper that steadily opposes anti-Semitism is accused of being Jew-inspired. Thus Mr. Belloc says (p. 202):

> A very marked example of it is a journal called *The New Republic*, which, though it has but a small proportion of Jewish writers upon it, and though its capital is (I believe) not Jewish, is yet to all intents and purposes the organ of the Jewish intellectuals, always joins in the boycott of any news unfavourable to European Jews, always joins in the clamour for anything favourable to them, and in general adheres to the Jewish side, like the *Humanité* in Paris, or, let us say, *The New Statesman* in England.

I may add to this that exactly the same charge could be brought against the *Church Times* which I have edited for the past nine years. And what is there in the charge? Only that newspapers that stand for justice and freedom and peace are compelled to defend the Jews, as they must defend all other people when they are unjustly accused, and to denounce cruelty and oppression.

It is often asserted that advertisers, as they supply the principal revenue of all newspapers, are able to dictate their policy. I have lived most of my life in newspaper offices, and I believe that this is utterly untrue. But even if it were true, in England the Jewish influence would again be negligible. Sir

DOES THE JEW MATTER?

Charles Higham—and no man speaks with greater authority—tells me that there is no advertising agency in Great Britain that is controlled by Jews, and that the great majority of advertisers in this country are Christian firms.

In America, since the death of the *New York World*, the *New York Times* is the only important Jewish-owned newspaper. It is quite impossible to get anything like accurate comparative figures, but I think it is true that the Jewish advertiser is more prominent in the columns of American newspapers than he is in England, but it is absurd to suppose that William Randolph Hearst, or the proprietors of such papers as the *Chicago Tribune*, determine their attitude to national and international problems to please the prejudices or to serve the interests of their Jewish advertisers.

M. Léon Dreyfus recently bought the Paris paper *L'Intransigeant*, but certainly not to benefit Jewry. No other important French newspaper is Jewish-controlled.

Until this year, on the other hand, in Germany several of the most important newspapers were owned by Jews and largely written by Jews. In Vienna, the *Neue Freie Presse* is a Jewish property and, before the war, practically every journalist one met in the Austrian capital was a Jew.

It would therefore seem that, if the Jews have used the Press for racial ends, they can only have done so in Germany, and again the reflection must be that they have shown precious little astuteness.

There is a further suggestion, for which there is some justification, that, in the dissemination of news by the great news agencies, there is a possibility of suppression, of exaggeration, and of absolute lying, that may and sometimes does lead to misunderstanding and to strife; and Mr. Belloc, with this in mind, has pointed out that von Reuter was a Jew; that Wolf, the founder of the German news agency, was a Jew; and that Jews have had a finger in the control of the Havas agency of France, and it is notorious that these three semi-official agencies have had a working arrangement with each other. But Reuters has had at its head now for many years Sir Roderick Jones, who is certainly not a Jew, and every journalist of cosmopolitan experience knows that the deficiency of the news agencies is that they are too much under the influence, not of the financier, but of the politician.

Havas, for example, has always sent out such news as the Quai d'Orsay has wanted the world to believe, and I have no doubt that the same thing occurs with Wolf, while Reuter takes part of the Havas and Wolf services. But the news agencies are largely affected by the messages sent by the newspapers' own correspondents in the various capitals, and no experienced newspaper man will be persuaded that in practice they have any considerable power for good or evil.

I turn from the right, from the capitalist and the money-grubber, to the left. Fear is overshadowing the councils of the nations—fear of neighbouring nations, fear of Communism, fear of Fascism, fear of bankruptcy—and the Red Terror has a portentous political influence. In the World Economic Conference in London, as in international conferences at Geneva, the representative of Russia has been the spokesman of the Red Terror, and he is a Jew. M. Litvinof is a stocky, solid man, mentally entirely Western, definite in statement and proposal, sardonically humorous, taking small pains to hide the contempt that a man who knows his own mind must have for men, many of whom seem to have no minds at all. He has the supreme advantage, when he comes into council, of possessing a clear-cut political philosophy. He knows exactly the goal at which he is aiming. Compromise and concession may at times be inevitable, but generally the Bolshevist is quite clear how the goal will be ultimately attained. The Red Terror is a reality in a world of make-believe, and to meet M. Litvinof is to understand something of the intellectual efficiency of its protagonists. And, as I say, M. Litvinof is a Jew! With M. Litvinof as its European plenipotentiary, it is easy to aggravate the suspicion that Bolshevism is a Jewish conspiracy against civilization.

Mr. Belloc says that "modern capitalism, by which the Jew has so largely benefited, but which he did not originate and in which prominent, though few, Jewish names were so inmixed, had for its counterpart and reaction the Socialist movement" (p. 62). This accurate statement is elaborated by that other distinguished Roman Catholic writer, Mr. Christopher Dawson. Karl Marx was not the father of modern Socialism. He was, as Mr. Belloc says, the pupil of Louis Blanc, but Marx "presented in complete form the full theory of Socialism, economic, social, and by implication religious, for he postulated Materialism," and Marx taught that Socialism was the inevitable end of *bourgeois* civilization. A member of the race that is the *bourgeoisie par excellence* foretold the end, or if you will, the ultimate development of the civilization, with which his race had been intimately concerned.

But it is certainly true that the Marxian philosophy has, as Lucien Wolf has said, "no relation to any recognised school of Jewish thought". And Bolshevism, as put into practice by Lenin, differs essentially from the Marxism of *Das Kapital*, which became in the last quarter of last century the Bible of European Socialists, most of whom had never read that heavy work.

Mr. Hilaire Belloc has well described Socialism as the "counterpart and reaction of modern capitalism", and Mr. Christopher Dawson quotes Dr. Gurain as declaring that "Bolshevism is at once the product of the *bourgeois* society and its judgment upon it; it reveals the goal to which the secret philosophy of that society leads if accepted with unflinching logic." Karl Marx taught that Communism must be the consequence of capitalism according to some almost divine law from which there was no possibility of escape. Mr. Belloc says that though the Jews did not originate the Socialist faith, "it rapidly fell more and more under their control", and that "after Karl Marx came a group of his compatriots who led the industrial proletariat in a rebellion against the increasing power of the capitalist system and began to organise a determined revolt". This statement is an evident exaggeration.

DOES THE JEW MATTER?

While Socialism in central Europe was, in its early stages, largely inspired by Jewish leaders such as Marx, Engels, Sanger, and Adler, these men, including Marx, in his maturity, were definitely evolutionary rather than revolutionary. Marx, says Mr. Lathrop Stoddart in his *Revolt Against Civilisation*, "came to believe that modern society was bound to work itself out into the Socialist order of his dreams with little or no necessity for violent compulsion, except perhaps in its latest stages".

After the revolution of 1848, there were two definite Socialistic schools. The first associated with the Russian, Bakunin, and the Frenchman, Proudhon, was opposed to all forms of government and repression. Bakunin wrote in his book *Dieu et l'État*, published six years after his death: "We object to all legislation, all authority and all influence, privileged, patented, official and legal, even when it has proceeded from universal suffrage, convinced that it must always turn to the profit of a dominating and exploiting minority against the interests of the immense majority enslaved." Both Bakunin and Proudhon would of necessity have been the fiercest possible enemies of the Bolshevist *régime* in Russia which professes to be Marxism in practice, even though it is Marxism radically modified. Against Proudhon and Bakunin, Marx and his school predicated a society in which equality, both political and economic, would be joined with authority and a willing submission to such laws and regulations as were found necessary for the common good. Here again was the contest between

the flamboyant and the drab, and here again, even in
the preaching of revolt against existing conditions, the
Jewish Socialist leaders remained inherently *bourgeois*.
If, therefore, there was any real reason for believing
that the right of the individual to possess property is
threatened or has been threatened by an organized
Jewish propaganda, it must also be recognized that
the substitute for capitalist society, envisaged by these
Jewish teachers, had certain qualities of organization
and practicability not to be found in the revolutionary
dreams of a Bakunin or a Proudhon.

But long before the end of last century the pure
milk of the Marxian gospel had been adulterated both
by political common sense and by sentimentality.
This was true in England, particularly, where the
Socialist movement, that grew, with great rapidity, in
the decade before the war, relied for its intellectual
justification on the cold logic of Lord Passmore, and
owed considerably more to the prophetic zeal of Keir
Hardie to whom it is fairly safe to assert Karl Marx
was no more than a name. In Germany the Social
Democratic Party was Marxian in philosophy, anti-
revolutionist in policy, and eminently *bourgeois* in its
timidity. Under the iron hand of Hitler it has ceased
to exist, and I am convinced that it will never experience a resurrection, for if, as many people like to believe but I most profoundly doubt, there is within
the next few years a reaction against the tyranny
of the Nazis, that reaction will most certainly be Communist.

Mr. Belloc says that " before the Great War one

could say that the whole of the Socialist movement, so far as its staff and direction were concerned, was Jewish '' (p. 53). And he goes on (p. 57): '' The Jews, with their perpetual movement from country to country, with their natural indifference to national feeling as a force counteracting class feeling, with their lucid thought and their passion for deduction, with their tenacity and intellectual industry, had naturally become the chief exponents and the most able leaders. They formed, above all, the cement binding the movement together throughout the world.''

I have already dealt with Mr. Belloc's odd illusion that the Jews are always folding their tents and constantly moving on, like a nation of ' Poor Jo's ' unimpelled by the police. I have already answered the charge that they are indifferent '' to national feeling ''. And if these suggestions are incompatible with the facts, so is the statement that, before the war, '' the most able leaders '' of the European Socialist movement were Jews. There was, as I have admitted, a large Jewish element in the German Social Democratic Party, but, while Singer was a Jew, the two best known leaders, Beber and Liebknecht, were not. The Frenchman, Jaurès, the most influential pre-war Socialist in Europe, was not a Jew. In Great Britain the Socialists have not had a single prominent Jewish leader. The old Social Democratic Federation, which claimed to stand for pure Marxism, was led by H. M. Hyndman, a portly and well-born English stockbroker. There was no Jew among the Fabian intellectuals. The Labour Party was largely a creation of Keir Hardie, and its pre-war leaders were Ramsay MacDonald and Philip Snowden. In the two semi-Socialist Governments since the war, there was only one Jewish Minister, and he held a subordinate position. It is simply not the fact that the pre-war European Socialist movement, deriving its inspiration more or less (generally less rather than more) from Marx, was predominantly Jewish.

But supposing that it were, and admitting (as I most certainly do not admit) that the Socialist movement is necessarily anti-Christian, here is indeed a story of the plot that failed. In Germany and Italy the Socialist parties have been destroyed. In France, the Socialists, led by Léon Blum, a Jew, are split into two factions, and are so fearful of a Fascist reaction that they have practically abandoned any attempt at a constructive policy. In Great Britain the Labour Party is pathetically impotent, and the Independent Labour Party an inconsiderable rump.

The war killed the influence of the Second International, the Social Democratic International. Fear of the Communists has largely prevented its resurrection. Ever since 1917 the Communists have waged war, both in Russia and outside it, against the Social Democrats whose moderation they have ridiculed and whose leaders they have constantly denounced. In so far as pre-war Socialism was Jewish, it has found in Communism its bitter enemy. If there had been an alliance between Socialists and Communists in Germany, Hitler might have been defeated in the election this spring. But as recently as last summer the Central Committee of the Communist Party issued a manifesto in which it was declared:

> In our policy as a whole, as well as in the election compaign, the main strategic consideration is still to direct *the main attack among the members of the working-class against the Social Democrats.* In face of the malicious calumnies of the class enemy concerning a supposed fundamental change in our strategy and tactics, we must make it clear to every Communist that the line of our class policy obliges us as our primary duty to isolate the Social-Democrats, to draw the workers away from them, since this is the most important preliminary condition for victory over our chief enemy, the bourgeoisie.— (*International Information. July 25th*, 1932.)

Socialism has, temporarily at least, ceased to be any sort of menace to the *bourgeoisie* and the established order. How far is Communism, which is a very real menace, Jewish? Mr. Belloc is very clear about it. He says:

> When in 1917 a socialist revolution was accomplished suddenly at one blow, in one great State, and when its agents, directors, and masters were seen to be a close corporation of Jews with only a few non-Jewish hangers-on (each of these controlled by the Jews through one influence or another), it was quite another matter. The thing had become actual. The menace to national traditions and to the whole Christian ethic of property was immediate.

A close corporation of Jews, presumably acting under the orders of the Elders of Zion! But, once more, what are the facts? The Jewish Bund was formed among the workers in the Russian Pale of

Settlement in 1897. At the beginning, it was mildly Socialist and at least semi-Zionist. Before 1905 the Bund had become allied with the revolutionary parties, and was prominently associated with the revolution of that year, paying its full share of the penalties consequent on its suppression. The Bund ceased to exist in Russia during the war, but it continued in Poland, a constitutional Socialist party with numerous representatives on local governing bodies.

Accepting Trotsky's contention that the failure of 1905 was the necessary education of 1917, and remembering that the Jewish workers were almost the only organized workers in Russia, they must bear part of the ultimate responsibility for the Bolshevist triumph. But in his brilliant history of the revolution Trotsky makes it clear that the immediate victory owed little or nothing to Jewish leadership. Years before the war the Russian Communist Party had split into two sections, the Bolshevists and the Mensheviks, the revolt against Lenin being led by the Jew, Markoff, with whom Trotsky himself was associated at that time. The bulk of the Russian Jewish Socialists were Mensheviks, and remained Mensheviks. In the early stages of the 1917 revolution, the Bolshevists realized that Menshevik moderation stood in the way of speedy and complete triumph, and in his history, Trotsky, who, in 1917, had become a confirmed Bolshevist, girds at the Petrograd Mensheviks as fiercely as he girds at Stalin. The Mensheviks were forcibly suppressed. The Bolshevists gained supreme power. And in 1917 there is no question that there were far more Jews among the Mensheviks than among the Bolshevists. The Jewish revolutionist paid for his moderation.

But what of Mr. Belloc's "close corporation of Jews" at the head of the Soviet State? In 1920, of the seventeen People's Commissars, only one—Trotsky—was a Jew by birth. There were, perhaps, a dozen other important Jewish Soviet officials, among them Zinovieff, who has held various offices, including the chairmanship of the Third International, Kameneff, Radek, Litvinof, Joffe, the first Soviet Ambassador to Germany, Rosengolz, who was for a time in London, and Rothstein, the Soviet Ambassador to Turkey. During Lenin's lifetime, Trotsky was the second most important personage in Russia, and it is not to be denied that Jews played an important and often a ruthless part in the establishment of the Bolshevist *régime*. But these effective agents of revolution cannot be regarded as forwarding the interests of Jewry. The Bolshevist Jew is, from the point of view of race and religion, an apostate Jew. Mr. Israel Cohen says (*Jewish Life in Modern Times*, p. 158):

With the accession to power of the Georgian Stalin and the subsequent fall of Trotsky, the influence of the Jews was reduced almost to nothing, and M. Litvinof is now the only Jew in high office, and outside his own department of Foreign Affairs, he has notoriously little or no influence. In 1926 it was officially stated that the Jews formed less than four per cent of the membership of the Communist Party, Russia's political aristocracy.

Jews are prominent in the lower ranks of the Soviet bureaucracy, but there is no more reason to suppose that they are all Communist than there is to suppose that every government clerk in Whitehall is a fervent supporter of the Nationalist Cabinet. Before the revolution the bulk of the Russian Jews were small traders, and while the Jewish artisan is accepted as a proletarian and shares his privileges, the trader was ruined. I again quote Mr. Cohen (*Jewish Life in Modern Times*, p. 191):

> The political revolution brought the Jews the civil liberty for which they had groaned for centuries, but the economic revolution has rendered it a far more trying problem for them to gain a living than under the most grinding laws of the Tsars. For the great mass of the Jews, until the advent of the Soviet Government, were either traders or small artisans, and as the Government abolished private trade and organized large-scale State industries as well as co-operative retail distribution direct to peasant villages, the Jews were deprived of their livelihood. For a short period it seemed as if they might be able to regain their positions. That was from the spring of 1921, when the 'New Economic Policy', commonly called 'Nep', was introduced, which restored legality to private commerce and industry, but this relief was but short-lived owing to the heavy taxation imposed upon private commercial and industrial establishments. By the end of 1923 the taxes had grown so heavy that many industries collapsed beneath them, and simultaneously the small Jewish trader found his business increasingly paralysed by the State's encouragement of consumers' and producers' co-operatives.

The Jew trader found his occupation gone, but the

Jew even in pre-revolution Russia, was nearly always literate, and he has naturally found employment as a smaller official, finding it politic and indeed necessary if he would avoid starvation to keep his religious and political opinions to himself. The Jews in western Europe may be growing indifferent to their religion, but the Jews in Russia were, before the revolution, notorious for their orthodoxy. Persecution has never succeeded in robbing the Jew of his faith, but it has sometimes been severe enough to induce him to pretend conversion. It is therefore improbable, if it is not inconceivable, that the mass of Jews in Russia, serving the Government or being obedient to its ordinances, are really apostate.

Jewry has gained nothing and can gain nothing from the establishment of Communism. If Stalin reigns in the Kremlin as the result of the machinations of Mr. Belloc's " close corporation of Jews ", then they have successfully contrived loss and suffering for their own people. But neither in theory nor in practice is Bolshevism Jewish. Its terrorism, its dictatorship of a minority, its adoption of force, are all Lenin's additions to Karl Marx. M. Litvinof is the Bolshevist spokesman in London, as other Jews have represented England in India, in Palestine, and years ago, in Berlin. But that they were selected for such responsibility is no proof that England was really governed by a "close corporation of Jews ", though perhaps Mr. Belloc believes that it is. Nor does the fact that the Soviet administration sends a Jew to an international congress prove that Jews are secretly pulling the strings in Moscow.

In 1923 there were three Jew Commissars, a Jew was President of the State Bank, and in the Ukraine a Jew was Commander-in-Chief of the army. Whether or not the Jewish influence is declining in the government of Russia, there is no question that the influence of Soviet Jewish officials is not exercised by them as Jews or for any discoverable definitely Jewish purpose.

An important aspect of the philosophy of Bolshevism is its repudiation of *bourgeois* morality. Traditional inhibitions are rejected as destructive of individual development and content, and thus inimical to the true interests of society. The charge that Soviet Russia has adopted the morality of the rabbit-warren is untrue. Promiscuity seems to be growing rarer, and there is among the younger Communists that austerity of conduct generally found in the earnest zealots of a new religion. Nevertheless, under Communism it is as easy to obtain divorce as to buy a postage stamp, the methods of birth-prevention are taught in public clinics, abortion is legal, and the institution of the family, regarded by Communist thinkers as a *bourgeois* anachronism, is being destroyed by the compulsory State employment of mothers and the State-care of children. To me the new morality is utterly damnable in its revolutionary attack on the bases of Catholic civilization, which derived so largely from the Jews. But its defenders have a case—indeed, a very strong case—if it be admitted that a man's life is actually "rounded in a sleep", that "to-day he is and to-morrow he is cast into the fire", and that is the end of him.

The new morality has its very able apologists in the

Western world. It has been advocated for the adolescent by Judge Lindsay in his plea for " companionate marriage ". It is more or less defended by H. G. Wells in the three volumes of *William Clissold*. It is expounded by Walter Lippmann in his *A Preface to Morals*, and by Bertrand Russell in his *Marriage and Morals*. The weary boredom of its practice is demonstrated by the novels of Aldous Huxley. I am convinced that Christian civilization is in greater peril to-day than it has been since Charles Martel defeated the Moors at the battle of Tours. If monogamy comes to be regarded as a harmful limitation of experiment and adventure, and the family is destroyed, then Christianity will be, temporarily, lost as the common inspirer of human action and self-control, and the Church will again suffer the apparent eclipse of the Dark Ages. And this may well happen.

If, therefore, the Elders of Zion, with their ears to the sound-board of the world, were constantly hatching plans for the overthrow of the existing order, it would be reasonable to suppose that Jews would be prominent among the teachers of the new morality. Lippmann is a Jew, but he is the only considerable Jew whose name occurs to me in this connexion. Probably Harold Laski, one of the most gifted of contemporary destructive thinkers, is in sympathy with Lippmann and Bertrand Russell, with a number of other Jewish intellectuals. But it would be preposterous to regard the new morality as a Jewish invention, or to hold Jews chiefly responsible for its propaganda.

There can, I think, be no doubt that the modern

pre-occupation with sex, with the resulting satiety and disappointment, has been stimulated by the theories of the psycho-analysts and their degradation of the purest of human instincts, and it has to be admitted that Jewish savants are prominent among the practitioners of psycho-analysis. The novels of Marcel Proust, a Jew, may condone and even encourage sex-preservation, but, for many reasons, Proust is far less pernicious than André Gide.

Certain distinguished Jews are concerned with this most important new morality movement, as certain Jews are concerned with all other modern movements. But it is again merely ridiculous to hold Jewry responsible for the new morality, particularly since it threatens the great institution which the Jews gave to society and which remains the most cherished of their possessions. The attack on the family must be dreaded by the great majority of modern Jews, at least as much as it is dreaded by nominal Christians. The family, says Israel Cohen, is " the stronghold of the Jewish sentiment ", and even among Jews, no longer moved by religious considerations, the family retains its traditional importance. As an example I recall the case of one of my Jewish friends, a pronounced unbeliever, who on no consideration will be away from his young sons on Friday evenings.

The destruction of the family is, as the Communist leaders quite properly realize, necessary before a Communist society can be brought into being. The existence of the family depends on life-long marriage and parental responsibility for the training and the welfare of the

children. "The home"—I again quote Israel Cohen
—"has been a characteristic of Jewish life from time
immemorial." So the Jewish family has been preserved. And the great majority of Jews can certainly
be counted on stoutly to resist the disintegrating
influence of the new morality in the society of which
they form a part.

It is unfortunate that Jewish opinion on this most
momentous issue is not more openly expressed. The
Jew can no longer shut himself in a water-tight com-
partment, comparatively indifferent to the life around
him. If his children do not marry Gentiles, as some of
them undoubtedly will, they must be affected by icono-
clastic theories, which may affect their lives even if
they are lived within the tribe. The family is the Jew's
gift to the world. He should make it quite clear that he
will stand shoulder to shoulder with the Catholic Church
in the fight for its preservation.

The Jews have no collective responsibility and a very
modified individual responsibility for the modern
revolutionary movement. Socialism has, to a considerable extent, been killed by its moderation. The Jews
have "an innate moderation", and in so far as they
were responsible for Socialistic leadership, this "innate
moderation" of theirs may be at least partly responsible
for Socialism's decadence. The same tendency caused
them in Russia to adhere to the Mensheviks, whom the
Bolshevists have destroyed. The Jew is, indeed, a complete failure as a revolutionist. He may march under
the Red flag, but it is generally with halting feet.

I have considered the Jews as a collective influence

in the modern world. I have shown the absurdity of supposing that they are responsible for the chaos in which we are living, for the subversive philosophy that may destroy the established order or for such plottings as actually occur for the fomenting of strife among the peoples.

The truth is that there is no such thing as International Jewry. Even Jews living in the same country and sharing the same interests find it always difficult and generally impossible to act together. International action, except for one definite purpose and for a short period, is almost unthinkable, so stubborn is Jewish individualism and so curiously common is his suspicion of his fellows. The Jews almost entirely lack the cohesion of the Irish.

In Great Britain there are no peculiar Jewish disabilities, and a Jewish political party or the organization of the Jewish vote, as the Irish vote is organized in many English constituencies, would be futile and foolish. In Poland the Jews suffer from legal disabilities, and are the victims of harassing administrative discrimination. They have the franchise, and they return Jewish members to the Seym, whose chief preoccupation should obviously be to fight, as the Irish fought for generations in the House of Commons, for the reform of the laws and their administration. But they are impotent because they are divided into warring sections. Mr. Israel Cohen, to whom I am so deeply indebted, had an article on the Jews in Poland in the *Jewish Chronicle* in April this year. In the course of it he said:

DOES THE JEW MATTER?

The Jews were represented in the first Seym by thirty-five deputies of their own, who were able to put up a strong fight against anti-Jewish tendencies, which became manifest from the very beginning. Since then, owing to Parliamentary reforms effected by the Government with a view to weakening the political power of the racial minorities, Jewish representation in the Seym had been reduced to ten. Had the Jewish deputies always been united they might have been successful in securing redress for the grievances of their people. But, unfortunately, they were divided from the very outset by differences both acute and complex, partly because of their dissonant standpoints within the Jewish community, and partly because of the varied outlook and mentality generated by the different regions from which they originated.

Thus, not only were there conflicts between the Zionists, the ' Bundists' (or Socialists), the 'Volkists' (or anti-Palestinian nationalists), the Agudists (super-orthodox anti-Zionists), and the assimilators (who wished to fuse quickly with the Poles without leaving a Jewish trace behind), but the Zionists themselves were divided as between Congress Poland and Galicia, for those living in the latter territory, being neighbours of the Ukranians (who were treated by the Government as potential insurrectionists) had views on the policy regarding the minorities contrary to those of their fellow-Zionists in Warsaw. Hence, the Jewish deputies often expended more energy, eloquence, and bitterness in attacking one another than in combating the common cause of all their woes.

What is true of Poland is also true of Latvia and Lithuania, and in a modified sense of Rumania and Greece.

Similarly at Zionist congresses there are always clashes of opinion concerning policy that do much to affect the growth of a great ideal. Even when Jewry is moved to righteous indignation as by the recent anti-Semitism in Germany, common action is only secured after the expenditure of infinite tact and patience. On Palm Sunday last a great meeting of protest was held under the auspices of the Jewish Friendly Societies in the Scala Theatre in London, and outside the theatre Jews, belonging to other organizations, were distributing handbills criticizing the over-moderation of the meeting's convenors. I imagine that the fear of certain entirely anglicized Jews of appearing to be more Jewish than English has something to do with this disinclination for common action, but the disinclination unquestionably exists, and it is one reason why the Jew matters so little.

The Jew never forgets that he is a Jew, but he is often anxious that other people should not always remember it.

The Jew in the British Parliament is concerned with British affairs. He must appear to his constituents as a good British citizen, which he is. It is not necessary that they should be moved to admiration by the fact that he is also a good Jew. If he sits for little Puddlington, it is essential that he should be more evidently concerned with the troubles of Little Puddlington's unemployed than with the sorrows of the Jews in Düsseldorf.

A man may quite properly be affected by two loyalties. All Catholics are. But sometimes there is a clash between the loyalties, as English Roman Catholics found in the reign of Elizabeth. And sometimes, for reasonable and honourable motives, a man may find it necessary to keep one allegiance to himself that he may fulfil the obligations of the other. This, I think, often happens to the Jew in western Europe, and it sometimes leads to an over emphasis of the second loyalty. This was illustrated by the Jewish novelist with an unmistakable German name, who fought through the war in the English army, and who, years after the war, declined to be present at a dinner given in London in honour of Gerhardt Hauptmann.

The same tendency is evident in the extraordinarily interesting career of the late Lord Melchett. In his biography, Mr. Hector Bolitho says strangely little of the fact that, but for Lord Melchett's enthusiasm for a cause in which it might be supposed he could have little personal concern, the Welsh Church would probably not have been disestablished. That the Church of Wales should have been attacked by Alfred Mond, as he then was, and defended by F. E. Smith, as he then was, is perhaps the most ironic circumstance in the modern history of Christendom.

The Jewish citizen's preoccupation with national affairs and his tendency to become *plus royaliste que le roi* leads him, so it is said, to comparative indifference to Jewish interests, though I am bound to add that this was by no means evident in the debates on the Nazi outrages in the Houses of Lords and Commons. But among their co-religionists there is a constant complaint that Jewish members of Parliament are timorous in " championing the cause of their own kith and kin ", and this timorousness, in so far as it exists, is sufficient

123

reply to the anti-Semitic suggestion that Lord Reading, Lord Bearsted, Lord Jessel, Lord Melchett, Lord Rothschild, Lord Swathling, Sir Herbert Samuel, Sir Percy Harris, Mr. Janner, Mr. Dudley Joel, Mayor Harben, Mr. James de Rothschild, Mr. Isidore Salmon, Sir Arthur Samuel, Mr. Samuel Samuel, Sir Philip Sassoon, Mr. E. A. Strauss, and Mr. Hore-Belisha are engaged in an international plot to establish a Jewish supremacy in the world.

I have set out the names of the Jewish members of the British Parliament as a comment on the common charge that Jews have an undue influence in the direction of public affairs. Of the six Jewish peers, Lord Reading has held high office under the Crown, and has been for years a great figure in public life. The other five are, in common with the majority of the Upper House, the comparatively undistinguished sons of their fathers. Of the twelve Jewish members of the Commons, again only one, Sir Herbert Samuel, is of Cabinet rank. Mr. Hore-Belisha and Sir Philip Sassoon hold subordinate positions in the National Government, and Sir Arthur Samuel was a minor Minister from 1927 to 1929. On the basis of population the British Jews are rather over-represented in the Commons. But the Jewish electors are nearly all town-dwellers, and on the basis of urban population the representation is certainly not excessive. Of recently deceased Jewish politicians, two exercised considerable influence in the conduct of affairs. I have referred to the late Lord Melchett. The late Edwin Montagu, as Secretary for India, acting in accord with the late Lord Chelmsford, the then Viceroy, took the first step towards Indian self-government, and thus may be said to have made history. Sir Herbert Samuel's excessive caution has made him a respectable but certainly not a great figure in British politics. His appointment as High Commissioner in Palestine was probably a mistake, and, though his administration was always correct, he was not an outstanding success. Certainly he could not be accused of excessive pro-Judaism.

Lord Reading had left politics before the war to become Lord Chief Justice, but his judicial office did not prevent him, in spite of tradition and owing to unprecedented difficulties, from taking an active behind-the-scenes part in the Government. He was constantly consulted by the Treasury, he was in the confidence of both Asquith and Lloyd George, and in 1918, in the momentous weeks before American intervention in the war, he went on a special mission to Washington. Since the war, he has been Viceroy of India, but, despite the fact that he is one of the ablest men of his generation, his Viceroyalty cannot be counted as of anything like the historic importance of the Viceroyalties of Lord Chelmsford and Lord Irwin.

Lord Reading is far more gifted as an observer and a critic than as a man of independent action. His prescience is illustrated by an entry in Lord Riddell's *Diary* in September 1918. Lord Reading had just returned from America and Lord Riddell writes as follows: " He views with apprehension commercial conditions after the war. He thinks the Americans will strive to scoop up the world's trade. The war has strengthened the Federal idea. America is becoming a great united nation, and as such will prove an even greater factor in the naval, military, and commercial life of the world." Here is certainly the acute observer, but the acuteness of judgment is not so apparent in his estimate of Woodrow Wilson as " a very wily, able man, who will take a great place in history ".

It cannot be pretended that Lord Reading has had any supremely important direct influence on the history of his age. Lord Irwin will be remembered in India generations after Lord Reading is forgotten. He has been a great advocate, a skilful politician, and a fairly successful judge. Indirectly his influence has been considerable. Politically, he has been by far the most influential Jew in Great Britain during this century, and his comparatively small importance gives the measure of Jewish influence.

D'Israeli, for all his inherited adherence to the Christian religion, was a flamboyant Jew and unquestionably made history, turning the smug England of Robert Peel into something like the colourful England of Elizabeth. Mr. Kipling is the singer of the England of Disraeli. He has had no successor in Jewry, or indeed in England. His Jewish successors in British politics have had none of his flair and his audacity. Many of them have been very able, all of them, with the possible exception of Edwin Montagu, have been drab.

Until recent years, the Jew has had no influence whatever in American politics. This is not, of course, surprising since he is a newcomer to America. During the war, however, Senator Baruch was appointed to the very important position of Chairman of the Industrial Board, and he remains an influential independent figure in Federal politics. For some years before the war the United States was generally represented in Constantinople by a Jewish diplomat, and since the war there have been several American Jewish ambassadors, the latest and most important appointment being that of Mr. Jesse Strauss to represent his country in Paris. For the first time a Jew became Governor of the State of New York at the last election, and there are now two or three other Jewish State Governors. But the Jew still has the feeblest of voices in American politics, and Jews have no power whatever in the determining of the international decisions of the American republic, though it should be added that two of the judges of the Supreme Court, the most influential judical body in the world, are Jews. One of them is Louis Brandeis.

In the British Commonwealth, a Jew represents the King in Australia, and in the last stage of the war the Australian army in Europe had a Jewish Commander-in-Chief. A dozen Jews perhaps have held high political and judicial positions in the Dominions and the Crown Colonies since the beginning of the century.

During this period no Jew has been of much importance in the *personnel* of the French Government, except, Lucien Klotz, and it was reported that Clemenceau said that he had appointed Klotz as his Minister of Finance because he was the only Jew in the world who knew nothing about finance. There have been Jewish ministers in Italy and in other European countries, none of whose names had any international significance. Only in Germany, and only since the war—Dernburg was born in the Christian faith—have Jews held predominant political office and have been in a position to initiate policy.

No one would deny that the Jews have made contributions of the greatest value to the intellectual and cultural life of the society of which they have formed a part for centuries. But the Jew's influence on thought and the Jew's contribution to the achievements of imagination are certainly not more than it would be reasonable to expect considering his numbers in the educated European communities. Spinoza and Bergson are the only two supremely great Jewish philosophers in the modern world, and Bergson's supremacy may well be questioned. Heine is the one great Jewish European poet. Georg Brandes, the Dane, is the one really important Jewish literary critic, and the list of Jewish imaginative writers—Disraeli, Israel Zangwill, Sidney Lee, G. B. Stern, Gilbert Frankau, Siegfried Sassoon, Humbert Wolfe, Philip Guedalla, in England; Marcel Proust and Catulle Mendès, in France; Schnitzler, Feuchtwanger, Wassermann, Emil Ludwig, Maxmilian Harden, and Max Nordeau, in Germany; Waldo Frank and Louis Untermeyer, and Walter Lippmann in America, suggest a high order of excellence, but, except in one or two instances, certainly not distinguished genius.

In the theatre in every country there have been

talented Jewish dramatists, men who knew their trade, of whom Alfred Sutro in England and Henri Bernstein in France are good examples, but whose work is hardly likely to have a continued existence; and even Max Reinhardt, regarded with considerable justification as the pioneer of a better and more imaginative play production, borrowed most of his ideas from Gordon Craig.

Similarly in the world of music where the Jew is most prominent, the Jewish composers—Mendelssohn, Meyerbeer, Offenbach, Halévy, Oscar Strauss—all men for whose inspiration the world has reason to be grateful, are not to be mentioned with the giants—Mozart, Bach, Beethoven, and Wagner. On the other hand, among executant musicians, Jews have always held distinguished and sometimes pre-eminent position— Joseph Joachim in the past, and Fritz Kreisler in the present, being perhaps the most eminent. In this connexion there is a curious and interesting example of Jewish adaptability and of his genius for producing the goods that are, at the moment, most in demand, two of the most successful composers of that jazz music which derives from negro tunes being Irving Berlin and George Gershwin, both of them American Jews.

In the arts one recalls the name of Joseph Israels, and Bakst the designer of scenery, and that great genius Joseph Epstein the sculptor. In the world of intellect, Einstein is a supreme world figure, and, as I have incidentally noted, the new psychology owed its origin to two Jews, Siegmund Freud and Carl Gustav Jung.

It is far from my purpose to attempt to minimize Jewish achievement. My intention is to demonstrate, that while the Jew is nearly always a useful and often a distinguished member of society, there is no such thing as a pre-eminence which should justify jealousy or be any cause for the belief that the Jew is intellectually endowed so far above the European average that Jewish domination of the world, as suggested in the *Protocols*, is a possibility to be feared. Regarded generally and with the whole gamut of the various forms of human activity in one's mind, it would be sufficiently true to say that on the whole, the Jew may be regarded as an excellent second-rater, and it is only very rarely that he contrives to get into the ranks of the first-raters in any form of human activity.

Walther Rathenau described the German people as "an association of interests and opposition". Jewry is hardly that, for it is not even an association. Now that anti-Semitism has again flamed into activity there is a new realization of brotherhood, but, in normal times and outside the ranks of the very recent immigrants, the Jew soon becomes much more conscious of himself as a citizen of the country in which he lives than as a member of a scattered and persecuted race. In his admirable little book on Zionism, Mr. Leonard Stein said of the Jews: " As their individual rights were enlarged, so their group consciousness tended to dwindle. They were still bound closely together by the ties of a common race and faith, but they no longer formed a well-defined and self-contained society. They had ceased to be simply Jews, and as Englishmen,

Frenchmen, Germans, or whatever it might be, they went their several ways." And it is as Englishmen, Frenchmen, Germans, that the Jews are important or unimportant in the world to-day.

The Jew everywhere is perfectly justified in being proud that Einstein is a Jew. But the Germans were equally justified, before they fell under the spell of Nazi insanity, in claiming Einstein as a German.

Unless he is absolutely faithless to his traditions, the Jew must in every country be opposed to those revolutionary movements that threaten personal liberty, personal property, and the social institutions that are the bases of the civilization which has developed during the past two thousand years. Therefore by the revolutionary of the right and by the revolutionary of the left, particularly perhaps by the revolutionary of the right, he is regarded as an enemy, but only as one of the rank-and-file in whatever army he marches. He will always be a minority of the rank-and-file. He will be a still smaller minority of the company officers. He will hardly ever be found in the highest command.

CHAPTER 4

ZIONISM

THE Jew, a nomad, " roaming from place to place for pasture ", against his will, by the force of circumstances, and not from any passion for perpetual motion, never ceases to dream of returning home, to the home from which he was banished for the last time in the year A.D. 131. In his book on Zionism, Mr. Leonard Stein says:

> The traditional attachment of the Jews to the cradle of their race and faith, their mystical belief in the final in-gathering, their wounded pride, their uneasy consciousness of a questionable status, their anxiety to regain their self-respect and to vindicate their right to self-expression, the outward pressure from the crowded Ghettoes of Eastern Europe, where half the Jewish race has lived for generations under the shadow of imminent danger—this is the complex of ideas, emotions and practical necessities which has gone to create the Zionist movement as it now exists.

But generations before the Jews had been finally scattered, only a minority of them lived in the Holy Land. There are said to have been about four million Jews in the Roman Empire, of whom only seven hundred thousand were in Palestine. The Jews were dis-

persed long before the Dispersion. But while the
Temple still stood in Jerusalem, the Holy City was
the place of pilgrimage. It was still home, and the
destruction of the Temple remains the most momentous
event in Jewish history. The Jews went on living in
the land of their fathers, under the Romans, after the
destruction of the Temple, under the Saracens, with
a large measure of happiness and content. Under the
Turks, there were always Jews in Galilee and Judæa.
But the home, at once religious and national, had disappeared and the Jews had become the homeless
people. In the middle of last century the Palestinian
Jews were a "poverty-stricken, dispirited community", reinforced every year by a trickle of immigrants from Russia and Poland, mostly old men, often
with young wives, yearning to die in the land of Abraham and Moses, not infrequently begetting extremely
ricketty children in the last years of their lives. The
Wailing at the Wall, that most moving of all the relics
left of ancient and medieval piety, summarized the
position of the Jews in Palestine. There was nothing
for them to do except to lament the days of the past.
" Ichabod, Ichabod, their glory has departed! "

The Jewish ache to return to Palestine naturally
grew considerably less when, after the French Revolution the Jew acquired citizen rights in many of the
countries in which he had settled, and began to find a
by no means unsatisfactory home away from home.
But sentiment is a stubborn thing. It always takes a
deal of killing, and the more or less assimilated Jews
of western Europe never could forget Zion. The idea

of a Jewish nation was largely lost. Many Jews, with commercial, political and sentimental attachments to the countries where they had made their homes were not unnaturally eager to forget that they were Jews by descent. But their neighbours never allowed them to forget. In England, during this century, the general attitude to the Jew has vastly changed. But until the past thirty years it was certainly true, as Mr. Leon Simon says in his *Studies in Jewish Nationalism*, that the assimiliated Jew was " an anomaly, Jew and non-Jew in one ". The Jews as a definitely separatist nation were only to be found in the ghettoes of eastern Europe. Mr. Leon Simon says:

> In the ghetto Jews have developed a form of life which is their own, determined primarily by their own national character; and that centre of Jewish life has been for over a century the great reservoir of Judaism, the source from which the scattered Jewish communities outside it have been able to draw something of Jewish feeling and Jewish culture. It is because of the existence of that centre of Jewish life that the Jew in lands of freedom is able to remain in some measure a Jew, to import some treasured relics of his own tradition into the non-Jewish life which he is compelled to live. But, much as the emancipated Jew owes to the ghetto, he is unable to look on it with respect and affection as the source of his Judaism and the standard expression of what Judaism should be, or to imagine himself returning to it in order to regain closer contact with his people. To leave the ghetto is to escape from slavery to freedom, from darkness to light; and no sane man would travel in the reverse direction.

A prison cell is never a satisfactory home, even

if the prisoner has his family with him. But it was the only home that the Jew was allowed. For him there was only one alternative, "either a cramped and stunted Jewish life in the ghetto, or the decay of Judaism and the Jewish consciousness under emancipation". But nineteenth century outbreaks of anti-Semitism proved that the prison wall provided no sort of security. The Jews of the ghettoes were harried and murdered. And the Jew who had escaped from the ghetto was given very clearly to understand that even those nations which had, in accord with democratic political theories, admitted him to citizenship would, if the alternative presented itself, infinitely prefer his room to his company. The consequence was a dramatic renewal of the Jewish consciousness and the quickening of the yearning to go home. This nineteenth-century homing spirit found one of its earliest expressions in a book written by Moses Hess, a German Jew, who lived for greater part of his life in exile in Paris, called *Rome and Jerusalem*, which was published in 1862. Hess declared that "it is only with the national rebirth that the religious genius of the Jews will be endowed with new strength and again be re-inspired with the prophetic spirit".

Modern Zionism may be said to have begun with the establishment of a Jewish agricultural school in Palestine in 1870. In the years that immediately followed, owing to the enthusiasm of Baron Edmond de Rothschild, various colonies of immigrants were settled in the country, and the movement passed from necessarily small efforts, subsidized by one philanthropist, into

a matter of world-wide concern, with the publication
in 1896 of *The Jewish State* by Theodor Herzl, who
expounded his ideas at a Jewish conference held at
Basle in 1897. Herzl's idea was to create a great
international organization of Jews to finance the establishment of a large Jewish settlement in Palestine, the
liberties of which should be guaranteed by the then
Turkish Government.

This was the ideal. But difficulties at once occurred.
Explaining what is known as the Basle Programme,
Mr. Leon Simon says:

> All that the aim of Zionism demands is first, that con-
> ditions favourable to the rebirth of Jewish national life
> shall be created in Palestine, and secondly, that the right
> attitude of mind shall be cultivated among the Jews
> throughout the world, so that numbers of them will be
> willing to become pioneers in the work of building up
> a Jewish life in the country. To bring into closer con-
> nexion the different bodies of Jews scattered over the
> globe, and to obtain recognition and assistance from the
> nations—these are subsidiary measures, however import-
> ant; and the possibility of carrying them out in practice
> depends entirely on the progress made in colonising
> Palestine and in reviving the Jewish consciousness. For
> only those Jews in whom the Jewish consciousness has
> been awakened will join a world-wide organisation of
> Jewry; and the extent to which Zionism can become a
> political force, capable of winning the sympathy and
> active support of governments, must be determined
> entirely by the strength of the Jewish holding in Palestine
> on the one hand, and the strength of the desire of the
> Jews for Palestine on the other.

The Turkish Government refused to give any of

the guarantees necessary if the scheme were to succeed. And despairing of any immediate settlement in Palestine, suggestions were made and favoured by certain influential Jews, among them, Israel Zangwill, the English novelist, for the establishment of a Jewish colony in British East Africa.

But to the Jew, most eager to leave Europe behind, Palestine was the only possible objective of a mass migration. For centuries he had been a city dweller. He knew how to scrape together a living in a city. In the East End of London, and the east side of New York, he could live in the conditions familiar in Warsaw and Lodz. Inspired by religious and national enthusiasm, he would make the long strange journey back to Palestine, but it was only in Palestine that he was willing to face life under entirely new conditions. He knew nothing of East Africa. But he had a " Palestine-sense ". To offer him the opportunity to return to Palestine was to provide the answer to centuries of prayer. Zionism was practical because it was intensely spiritual.

But for years little that was practical was effected. Herzl died in 1904 and Max Nordau, the German alienist, became the most conspicuous of the Zionist leaders. After the Turkish revolution, negotiations were carried on with the Young Turks, who promised much and gave little, and there was a small Jewish emigration into Palestine. But nothing of any great importance happened until the outbreak of the Great War. Mr. Stein says that there were eleven thousand Jews in Palestine in 1839, thirty-four thousand in 1878, and a hundred thousand in 1914. The Jewish Colonization Association, which owed a great deal to the beneficence of Baron Hirsch, came into existence before the war, and in 1914 there were forty-three agricultural Jewish colonies with holdings of about a hundred thousand acres. One important point has to be noted. Even in these early days, Hebrew—now one of the three official languages of Palestine—had become (I quote Mr. Stein) " the language not only of the synagogue and the seminary, but of the home and the school ".

To Herzl, Zionism was the Jews' reply to anti-Semitism, one more attempt to find the security which has been the Jews' constant search. He was a journalist, a man with a definitely practical mind, convinced by the Dreyfus trial that something must be done to save his race. Since Herzl's death Zionism has grown more romantic. It would be quite untrue to suggest that the western Jew, who supports the Zionist cause, is unaffected by its practical consideration and is not primarily concerned that his fellows should be able to live as free men and not as helots, constantly exposed to outbreaks of racial savagery; but Zionism has certainly found its driving force in the desire to provide " a home for the Jewish spirit ". This ideal affects tens of thousands of Jews, who have not the remotest idea of abandoning their comfortable material homes in Great Britain or France, or America. The ideal has been expressed by Asher Ginzberg, who wrote:

A national spiritual centre of Judaism to which all Jews will turn with affection, and which will bind all

138

Jews together; a centre of study and learning, of language
and literature, of bodily work and spiritual purification; a
true miniature of the people of Israel as it ought to be . . .
so that every Hebrew in the Diaspora will think it a
privilege to behold just once the centre of Judaism and
when he returns home will say to his friends: ' If you
wish to see the genuine type of a Jew, whether it be a
Rabbi or a scholar or a writer, a farmer or an artist or
a business man—then go to Palestine and you will see it.'

Long before immigration on a large scale was possible
the cultural aspiration found its expression in the proposal, made in 1913 by Dr. Weizman, for the establishment of a Hebrew University in Jerusalem for the development and the preservation of Jewish learning,
eventually to become '' the crowning glory of the Jewish
national home ''.

The Balfour Declaration was the beginning of post-
war Zionism. It was the result of protracted negotiations
between Zionist leaders and the British Government.
Dr. Weizman had been on the teaching staff of Manchester University, and through the good offices of C.
P. Scott, the famous editor of the *Manchester Guardian*,
as the representative of the Zionist leaders he began conversations with British Ministers in December, 1914.
Definite proposals were made in 1916, but it was not
until 1917, and then largely owing to the late Sir Mark
Sykes, who had an intimate knowledge of the Middle
East, that an agreement was made for the Jewish colonization of Palestine. In a letter to Lord Rothschild
on November 2nd, 1917, Mr. Arthur Balfour, as he
then was, said:

THE JEW TO-DAY

I have much pleasure in conveying to you on behalf of His Majesty's Government the following declaration of sympathy with Jewish Zionist aspirations, which has been submitted to and approved by the Cabinet:

"His Majesty's Government view with favour the establishment in Palestine of a national home for the Jewish people, and will use their best endeavours to facilitate the achievement of this object, it being clearly understood that nothing shall be done which may prejudice the civil and religious rights of existing non-Jewish communities in Palestine or the rights and political status enjoyed by Jews in any other country."

I should be grateful if you would bring this declaration to the knowledge of the Zionist Federation.

It should be noted as an example of the Jews inability to agree together that the agreement was hotly opposed by the two most important Jewish societies in England, who denied that Jewry possessed " a national character in a purely political sense."

The Declaration was backed by the Governments of France, Italy, and the United States, and approved by the League of Nations in 1922, when the Mandate for Palestine was accepted by the British Government, which, at the same time, undertook responsibility for " the establishment in Palestine of a national home for the Jewish people ". Exactly what this meant was carefully explained in a British statement of policy:

When it is asked what is meant by the development of the Jewish National Home in Palestine, it may be answered that it is not the imposition of a Jewish nationality upon the inhabitants of Palestine as a whole, but the further development of the existing Jewish community, with the assis-

140

tance of Jews in other parts of the world, in order that it may become a centre in which the Jewish people as a whole may take, on grounds of religion and race, an interest and a pride. But in order that this community should have the best prospect of free development and provide a full opportunity for the Jewish people to display its capacities, it is essential that it should know that it is in Palestine as of right and not on sufferance. That is the reason why it is necessary that the existence of a Jewish National Home in Palestine should be internationally guaranteed, and that it should be formally recognised to rest upon ancient historic connection.

This, then, is the interpretation which His Majesty's Government place upon the Declaration of 1917, and, so understood, the Secretary of State is of opinion that it does not contain or imply anything which need cause either alarm to the Arab population of Palestine or disappointment to the Jews.

For the fulfilment of this policy it is necessary that the Jewish community in Palestine should be able to increase its numbers by immigration. This immigration cannot be so great in volume as to exceed whatever may be the economic capacity of the country at the time to absorb new arrivals. It is essential to ensure that the immigrants should not be a burden upon the people of Palestine as a whole, and that they should not deprive any section of the present population of their employment. Hitherto the immigration has fulfilled these conditions.

Incidentally it should be mentioned that the Balfour Declaration of 1917 was followed in 1918 by the arrival in Palestine of two Jewish battalions to serve in Lord Allenby's army. One of these battalians was commanded by Colonel Frederick Samuel, D.S.O., and in them there were a large number of Jews who had been

recruited in the United States. Their arrival in the
Holy Land naturally aroused considerable enthusiasm,
and a locally-enlisted third battalion was subsequently
formed.

The Jews in Palestine suffered severely during the
war, and their numbers decreased by almost fifty per
cent, and it was not until 1920 that anything like a considerable Jewish immigration began. The immigrants
were then, as they are now, recruited as to ninety per
cent from eastern and from south-eastern Europe,
hardly any of them coming from the English-speaking
countries.

The present position in Palestine is set out in a recently
published and very elaborate report of the Palestinian
Government, which contains a careful analysis of the
population in November 1931. The total population of
the country, which was 750,000 in 1920, has increased
to over a million. The number of Jews settled in the
country has increased from 86,000 to 175,000. Half the
Jews now settled in Palestine were born in other countries. There has been a certain immigration of Arabs
into Palestine from Transjordania and Syria, with a
certain emigration of Christian Arabs to America, but
the increase in the Arab population has been mainly due
to natural causes. The Jews now constitute eighteen
per cent of the total settled population.

Even in Palestine the Jews largely remain city
dwellers. Despite the flourishing agricultural colonies,
three-quarters of the Palestinian Jews live in the towns,
which since the beginning of the British administration
have largely increased in population. Jaffa with its

modern sister-town, Tel-Aviv, the only hundred-per-
cent-Jewish town in the world, has increased in population from 45,000 to 100,000. The population of Jerusalem has increased from 50,000 to 90,000, and of Haifa
from 25,000 to 50,000. There is no increase in the population in the purely Arab towns though the Arab population has increased in the towns that are partly Jewish, and also in those parts of the country that are
being developed by Jewish capital and enterprise. My
own study of this most interesting official report entirely confirms Mr. Norman Bentinck's conclusion that
"it is abundantly clear that immigration and Jewish
enterprise are making the country more liveable for
the old as well as the new population".

There is a striking difference between the characteristics of the Arabs and the Jews. Seventy-five per cent
of the Arabs are peasants; seventy-five per cent of the
Jews are traders, artisans, or belong to the professional
class. Ninety per cent of the Jews are literate. Only
twenty-five per cent of the Arab men and ten per cent
of the Arab women are literate.

There is little unemployment in Palestine. In 1931
the Jewish unemployed were one per cent of the
Jewish urban population and two-fifths per cent of
the Jewish rural population. According to a Memorandum issued by the Jewish Agency for Palestine in
in June, 1932:

No reliable statistics with regard to unemployment
among Arabs, urban or rural, are available. The statistics
sometimes given, indicating Arab unemployment ranging

between 12,000 and 35,000, according to season, are
based on computations made by *mukhtars* of villages,
and are admitted to include, not only ' unemployed ' in
the ordinarily accepted sense of the term, but also large
numbers of small farmers, or tenant-farmers, who are
accustomed to seek paid employment in the slack season.
No adequate machinery at present exists for the compila-
tion of a reliable register of Arab unemployment, and the
figures given should therefore be accepted with reserve.

The suggestion that the Jew can never, with the
ghetto generations behind him, become a successful cul-
tivator is disproved by this Memorandum, which says:

Palestine agriculture has naturally not escaped the consequences of the world-wide depression and fall in prices
of agricultural commodities, but it has, on the whole,
suffered less than other countries, since a large proportion
of its agricultural produce is sold in the home market.
The settlements engaged in dry-farming were most
severely affected by the depression while the plantation
settlements (which account for some 60 per cent of the
Jewish rural population) continued to make steady progress in spite of adverse conditions. . . . The total Palestinian orange export for the 1931–32 season is one of the
largest on record, amounting to more than 3,000,000 cases,
of which more than two-thirds came to Great Britain.
Exports of grape-fruit, begun in 1929–30 with a shipment
of 17,000 cases, rose in the 1931–32 season to 70,000
cases. Like the Jaffa orange, Palestinian grape-fruit finds
a ready market in England, and markets abroad, e.g. in
Germany, show a steady tendency to expand.

The Jew in Palestine remains the *bourgeois*, always
desirous of working for himself rather than working for

wages, and the Zionist authorities are satisfying this racial yearning by the encouragement of small holdings, but only when the potential small holders have acquired technical knowledge. I quote from the Memorandum:

> During the past few years numbers of *Halutzim* ('pioneers') have settled in the neighbourhood of the principal plantation villages, and, working as labourers on the estates of the larger planters, have become expert in the various branches of citriculture. Many of them, while still living in barracks, started small nurseries of orange or grape-fruit trees on their own initiative, or devoted their spare time to market-gardening or dairying on a small scale. It was felt that the time had come to afford these people an opportunity of establishing themselves permanently on the land, and a scheme has accordingly been worked out. . . .
>
> The Jewish National Fund has acquired substantial areas of land in the vicinity of the principal plantation settlements, and this land will be devoted to the establishment of these experienced agricultural workers as smallholders. Each approved settler under the scheme, up to the number of 1,000 in the first instance, will receive a cottage with a large garden irrigated for vegetable-growing, etc., and $7\frac{1}{2}$ dunams of irrigated land suitable for citrus growing, together with the necessary initial credits for installation, and development expenses. . . . It is anticipated that the settlers under this scheme will continue to work for larger planters until their own groves reach bearing-age (about five years), and that many of them will continue to do so afterwards.

I find it impossible to arrive at exact figures of the Jewish capital invested in Palestine since the beginning of the British mandate. But the economic condition of the country is remarkably satisfactory, and the facts justify the assertions of Mr. Nahum Sokolow, the President of the Jewish Agency who, writing in September 1932, said: " Palestine is probably one of the few countries, the public revenue of which does not reflect the crisis which has forced governments of other countries into policies of drastic retrenchment. It is generally recognized that this is mainly due to the large funds flowing into Palestine as a result of Jewish settlement work, and to the steady development of agricultural and industrial enterprise by groups of, and by individual, Jews."

The most important industrial development in Palestine is the extraction of mineral salts from the Dead Sea, which has now passed the experimental stage. As Mr. Norman Bentwich says: "Within a few years Palestine promises to be one of the principal chemical-producing countries of the world; and the Dead Sea is its inexhaustible reservoir." This means increasing general employment and increasing wages for Arabs as well as Jews.

Agriculture is being modernized, and the peculiar qualities of the country are beginning to be exploited. New orange groves are being planted. I quote from Mr. Mills: " The growing of vegetables has developed considerably during the past few years . . . ; cultivation of grapes among the Jews has been developed mainly for the manufacture of local wines, but of recent years great progress has been made in supplying table grapes and the varieties most attractive in appearance and in

taste; the cultivation of apricots, peaches, and nec-
tarines has also developed considerably in recent
years."

There is obviously room and need for further immigration, though the Government is still—in view of Arab
fears—regulating and restricting the immigration.

There is one section of the official report to which I
have referred that, from the purely British point of view,
certainly justifies the policy of the Balfour Declaration.
Reconstruction has made Haifa the second port in importance in the Eastern Mediterranean. Pipe-lines are
being laid from Haifa to the oil-field in Kirkuk, with a
railway running alongside, and Haifa, under British
control, is destined to be one of the centres of the oil
trade. The Balfour Declaration was not dictated by any
love for the Jews. Primarily it was intended to attract
Jewish goodwill, particularly in America. Secondarily
it was intended to secure for Great Britain the control of
one of the gates of the East, given an ever-increasing
importance by the oil-fields, and by the development
of aviation traffic between Europe and Asia. From
the narrow British point of view, the Balfour Declaration has been abundantly justified.

From the Jewish point of view, remembering the
spiritual and intellectual ideal of Zionism, I find most
significance in the statistics relating to the languages
habitually spoken to-day in Palestine. Mr. Mills, the
compiler of the report, warns the student that the figures
suggesting the revival of Hebrew as " the medium of the
expression of life "—the number of persons habitually
speaking Hebrew is said to have doubled in the years

from 1922 to 1931—are not altogether reliable. But he goes on:

Although the census statistics may be unreliable, there are other grounds for supposing that the development of Hebrew among the Jews in Palestine during the last ten years is remarkable, not only in its quantitative aspect as a vehicle of ideas, but also in its vital aspects, that is, in its adaptation to the needs of modern life. The importance of this may be judged from the following illustration. I have been told that some Jewish children in pre-war Palestine, brought up in households where Hebrew alone was spoken, suffered emotionally and intellectually, because the development of Hebrew had not kept pace with the development of the human being. Twentieth century children were unable to find complete self-expression in language adapted to the needs of the fifth century B.C. and suffered, as children will, when not able to release themselves through the extravagances of speech habitual to their age. Language is born of human laughter and tears, and developing civilization has greatly extended the gamut of the emotions.

Another interest may lie in the fact that while the perceptual idea underlying a word, that is its denotation, may be identical in different languages, the conceptual idea, that is, the connotation may be different. The revival and development of a language, in general confined for centuries to liturgical and devotional expression, may, therefore, open new avenues of thought and research into the activities of life, provided that the development is natural and not too heavily weighted by artificial borrowing from the developed languages. On the other hand, while Hebrew may become the *lingua franca* of the Jews, it is likely to remain for non-Jews a language the acquisition of which will only be necessary for certain types of scholars; so that Jews, engaged in the ordinary affairs of the world, will probably be compelled to maintain their honourable and justified reputation for poly-lingualism. This observation is realized by the Jews in Palestine since, in most Jewish schools, some Arabic is taught to enable the members of the coming generation to converse freely with their neighbours, and, in many schools, opportunity is given for learning at least one European language. The difficulty of reconciling the claims of a curriculum, such as educationists would normally approve, and the claims to be acquainted with languages, other than that of the medium of instruction, presents a problem demanding sympathetic interest.

Another phenomenon which deserves attention is the growth of Hebrew as a secondary language among Arabs. No measure of this growth is given by the statistics which relate only to the languages in habitual use. The traveller through rural Palestine, however, will not fail to notice that in the sphere of economic activity, for example in orange cultivation and in motor transport to and from Jewish villages, local Arabs are finding it advantageous to converse freely with their Jewish neighbours in Hebrew. Arabic and Hebrew, being of the Semitic family, have definite affinities, and it appears that those Arabs, who find its use of economic advantage, learn quickly to speak Hebrew correctly. Parallel with this special bi-lingual development is the movement among both Arabs and Jews to acquire English as a secondary language: this movement finds expression among the Arabs in urban centres, and among Jews in both the urban and rural populations.

Mr. Leon Simon says: " Palestinian Hebrew litera-ture touches the actual problems of life at more points than does the Hebrew literature of the Diaspora. It is concerned with questions of agriculture, of pædagogy, of industrial development, which can scarcely come within the scope of an author who is not himself in Palestine and does not write specially for Palestinian readers. And thirdly, in the domain of poetry and *belles-lettres* it is open, as Hebrew literature elsewhere is not, to the influences of Palestinian scenery and life and of the historic memories of which the land is so full."

It would, therefore, seem from the highly significant passage that I have quoted from Mr. Mills's report, that in Palestine to-day there is occurring the gradual revival of a nation that, in its culture and its direction is distinctively Jewish.

The Arabs will always have, at least while the British mandate continues, equality in citizenship, but as culturally they are generations behind the Jews, it would seem inevitable that, even granted nominal equality of citizenship, they must inevitably be, for the most part, the hewers of wood and the drawers of water. The Arabs certainly fear a Jewish domination. The outbreaks two years ago were evidence of that fear. And no one will doubt that, but for the British administration, there would be the probability of constant trouble. But, as a matter of fact, the Arabs have everything to gain from the Jewish immigration. Palestine is sparsely populated and is, in effect, as Mr. Leonard Stein says, " a derelict country ". Jewish capital and Jewish enterprise must provide lucrative employment for the Moslem majority and raise their standard of comfort.

Honour and self-interest compel Great Britain to keep her pledges to the Jew, and ultimately the Balfour Declaration must obviously be to the advantage of the entire population, even though the arrival of keen-minded Jews may temporarily affect the interests of the Christian Arab trader and of the small class of Moslem *intelligentsia*. The fact, officially noted, that the Arabs are beginning to learn Hebrew is sufficient proof that they are beginning to appreciate the advantage of association with the Jews.

Sooner or later, Zionism must mean a predominantly Jewish Palestine. I see no advantage in ignoring so very obvious a fact. From my own observation, I should agree that the country can support a population of about three millions—that is, three times its present population. There have been some 100,000 Jewish immigrants during the past twelve years. The Government is granting this year 11,000 certificates for assisted immigrants. This was accepted as the yearly maximum, and even if the number were considerably increased by the immigration, at present unrestricted, of persons with means, it is clear that it must be many years before the maximum population is reached.

But in view of the possible consequences of the organized anti-Semitism in Germany, it is necessary to have the Zion idea clearly in mind. In his book from which I have quoted, Mr. Leonard Stein says:

The Jews are almost everywhere unhappy and uncomfortable. Where they are not persecuted, they are nevertheless acutely conscious that as a body they are disliked. There is hardly a country in the world in which a Jew is not, as such, under impalpable but well-recognised disadvantages. Even where the Jews are least unwelcome they are perpetually on the defensive. They are, in fact, suffering from what may almost be called a minority complex. In Jewish self-pity there is, needless to say, an element of morbid exaggeration. But the broad fact remains that the Jews are hardly anywhere at ease. Surrounded, as they think, by a world of enemies, they see in Palestine the symbol of their will to live.

But their desire is not merely to live, but to live at peace with the world. They are perpetually accused of being parasites. They are told that they can imitate but cannot create. The taunt is unjust, but it stings. It is in Palestine that the Jews see their opportunity of making their distinctive contribution to the common stock. Here is a derelict country in which everything remains to be done. Let the Jews rebuild it; let them reclaim its wastes; let them develop its neglected resources; let them make it a model of a healthy and well-ordered society; let them give it a place of its own in the world of thought and learning. Then, indeed, they will have triumphantly vindicated themselves as a constructive force.

Thus what the Jews are doing in Palestine is to translate spiritual values into terms of economic reconstruction. And in another and a profounder sense the Jews, in redeeming Palestine, are redeeming themselves.

I have considered some of Mr. Stein's exaggerations. It really is not the fact that the Jew is " hardly anywhere at ease ". It is not the fact that " they are surrounded by a world of enemies ". It is certainly not true that they are generally " accused of being parasites ". But, with all his rhetorical exaggeration, Mr. Stein does explain the Jewish yearning for Palestine. To Mr. Stein I add Mr. Israel Cohen, who writes:

ZIONISM

The colonization of Palestine, inspired by a national purpose, hallowed by religious tradition, and directed towards an ideal end, will extend its beneficent influence throughout the dispersion, acting as a bulwark even to some distant community thousands of miles away that might otherwise be exposed to the corroding forces of its environment. By the subtle links that are slowly forged between such a community and the new Judæa will its members be preserved from absorption—by their personal share in the labours of the Renaissance, by periodical pilgrimages to its principal centres, by studying its intellectual products and furthering its welfare in thought and deed.

The new Judæa cannot contain the whole of Jewry, nor will most of the Jews of the West be willing to exchange the comforts and amenities of their homes for the comparative simplicity of the Land of Israel; but upon the success of its development will depend the survival of the Jewry beyond its borders. For in the face of the countless forces of assimilation to which modern Jewry is increasingly exposed, nothing can save it from slow and sure dissolution but the spiritual invigoration that it can receive from a national settlement. The sooner it realizes this pregnant truth, and the sooner it applies it by a continuous extension of practical and liberal co-operation, the larger and the more creative will be the potentialities of the Jewish National Home; and then perchance the dream that was dreamed throughout the centuries of exile and that seemed, in the first glow of imagination fired by the Balfour Declaration, suddenly to take visible shape, may yet become a concrete and glorious reality.

Both Mr. Stein and Mr. Cohen have the same objective. They envisage a purely Jewish State. Its language is to be Hebrew. Its religion is apparently to be

orthodox Judaism. Its university is to be the home
and the inspiration of a distinctive Jewish culture.
Although it can never be the home of more than a minority of the world's Jews, it is to be the Jewish home.
I fully understand the fineness of the ideal. I know how
intensely it is felt even by men who have no intention of moving permanently from Hampstead to
Haifa.

But the Jewish economic and finally the inevitable
Jewish political control of Palestine must, as it seems to
me, have as their consequences a profound and, as I
anticipate, unexpected effect for Jewry and possibly
serious and equally unexpected international reactions.
Hitherto the immigrants have mainly come from the
most harassed and the most orthodox section of Jewry,
the section least attracted by the culture of the West.
There is among them a percentage of young men and
women with Bolshevist and anti-religious sympathies.
But for the great majority, in these days, shut out of
America and Great Britain, immigration to Palestine
has been an escape from the present to the past. They
are back in the land of their fathers, living in infinitely
better conditions than they have ever lived in before.
They have actually lived " surrounded by a world of
enemies ". Now they are favoured by the authorities.
They find that to be a Jew is to have not disabilities
but privileges. The most intelligent of them have en-
thusiastically learned to express their everyday
thoughts in Hebrew, and to enable their children to
have their full share of the Hebrew culture enshrined
in the university on Mount Scopus. The ultra-conser-

vatives may cling to the familiar Yiddish, and yearn
(I once more quote Mr. Mills) '' to preserve Hebrew as
a language of liturgy and devotion, in which, as in a
casket, is enshrined the crystal of their faith ''.   But
they are a dwindling minority.

The character of the immigration into Palestine must
be affected by political events in central Europe.   The
funds being raised all over the world for the help of
the Jews in Germany, who have been robbed of their
livelihood by the Hitler revolution, will naturally be, to
a considerable extent, spent in assisting emigrations to
Palestine in so far as the quota, permitted by the British
administration, will allow.   For the next few years
I assume that the assisted emigrants will be largely German, while hitherto they have been almost exclusively
Russian and Polish.   A movement, too, has begun—
and will, I suppose, considerably increase—for German
Jews, possessed of a certain amount of capital, and
who are therefore not affected by the quota regulation,
to make their homes in Palestine. Taking the figures of
the past few years as a standard, it is possible that there
may be a German-Jewish immigration into Palestine of
6,000 persons a year, and at the end of ten years,
allowing for births, there may be 70,000 to 80,000 German Jews settled in the country, with possibly a considerable German-Jewish colony in Transjordania.   In
ten years' time, therefore, the Jewish population of
Palestine may be 300,000, of whom at least a quarter
will be Germans.   I am, of course, assuming that there
will be no change in the immigration policy of the
British administration, and that the vastly increased

immigration which the Zionist leaders demand will be refused.

The mentality and the average culture of these German immigrants will be vastly different from that of the immigrants from eastern Europe. I have noted that the German Jews are far more German than English Jews are English, and they are certainly far more German than the Polish Jews are Polish. They are the heirs of German culture, in the creation of which they have played a great part, and, however bitter they may be against the present German Government, and however properly resentful of the treatment to which they have been subjected, they will carry all the definite and distinguished qualities of German Judaism with them to Palestine, as the Pilgrim Fathers carried all the definite and distinguished qualities of English Puritanism with them to America.

The German Jew has nothing like the same devotion to his ancient religion as the Jews of the Pale. His language is German, and I should suppose that it will be immensely difficult to persuade him to abandon a language, in which there is a mighty literature, and to adopt Hebrew as his *langue du foyer*. Nor will the Hebrew University, in which the lectures are delivered in what to the new immigrants is exclusively a liturgical language, attract men whose fathers have been educated in one or other of the great German universities. This attitude seems to be suggested by Dr. Einstein's refusal to accept a professorial chair in the Mount Scopus University.

Culturally, the influx of Germans into Palestine must

fundamentally affect the *timbre* of the Jewish population, and at the same time add to the difficulties of
the government. It now has to deal with Moslem Arabs,
Christian Arabs, and Jews. It may have to deal with
Moslem Arabs, Christian Arabs, Polish Jews and
German Jews. If this difficulty is anticipated, the administration will be still more determined to limit the
number of Jewish immigrants.

I see no reason whatever for supposing that for some
years there will be any radical change in the anti-Semitic
policy of the German Government. The Hitler decrees
have already stimulated anti-Semitism in Hungary, in
Austria, in Poland, and in Rumania. It is therefore reasonable to fear that the Jews are at the beginning of
another tragically troubled period in their always
troubled history, with the consequent quickening of the
yearning for an *enclave* of their own where at least a
portion of the Jewish population of the world may be
safe from their enemies. This must mean that great
pressure will be brought to bear on the British Government so to alter its policy as to hasten the day when
Palestine will be predominantly Jewish, but I should
think it probable that not unreasonable fear on the part
of the Government and the impossibility that the Jews,
as I have noted, always find in acting together in anything for but the briefest period, will combine to prevent any speedy realization of what is at once a great
ideal and a great necessity. Consequently Zionism, important as it is to the Jews, and intensely interesting as
it is to the whole world, offers little practical protection
against anti-Semitism.

CHAPTER 5

THE JEWISH RELIGION

IF the Jews entirely lose their religion, their existence
as a separate community will swiftly come to an end.
That is an assertion often made, and I think that is true.
" Israel was once a nation; it is now a Church," says
Mr. Claud Montefiore. And Mr. Montefiore argues that
if Jewish nationalism could be purged of religious texts
and disabilities the purgation would mean the disappearance of Judaism. The very interesting men concerned with the spread of Liberal Judaism are influenced
primarily perhaps by devotion to the Jewish faith and to
the essentially Jewish conception of God, but certainly
they are influenced secondarily by the belief that Jewry
cannot exist without the Jewish religion, and that, therefore, this religion must be adapted to modern discoveries
and to modern thought. Their position is almost exactly
that of the Christian Modernists, and between the Rabbi
Mattuck and Dr. Major there is certainly no great gulf
fixed. Mr. Claud Montefiore says in his tract, " Some
Rough Notes about Liberal Judaism " :

> In the belief that Orthodox Judaism, as a religious
> whole, has broken down, and that only fragments, dis-
> parate and unharmonized, are left, Liberal Judaism is an

158

attempt to make Judaism a living, working religion. harmonious and consistent in all its parts.

It may be asked: Why has Orthodox Judaism broken down? Or: In what respects has it broken down?

It has broken down doctrinally. The newer criticism of the Bible has made the position upon which it rests of a homogeneous, Mosaic law untenable. Again, it has broken down philosophically. The Law is not only not Mosaic, but it is not, in the old, orthodox sense, divine. No book, no Code, is, in the old, orthodox sense, divine. Again, it is not, in the old, orthodox sense, morally and religiously perfect. It contains a mixture of very good and very true; less good and less true; and what is, for us, not good or true at all. Our conceptions of Revelation and of Inspiration in relation to the Pentateuch have moved much beyond the conceptions of Maimonides. . . .

Our conception of the place of women in religion is very different from the conception of orthodoxy. Nor can we approve of many orthodox rulings about Divorce and the Laws of Marriage. The distinction between Priest (Cohen) and Layman has become for us meaningless and even objectionable. Any idea of the re-establishment of animal sacrifices in a Messianic (!) age is to us revolting. The true nature of old and priestly ideas about outward purity, and of primæval taboos about food, has been revealed to us by historical investigations, and our attitude to the Pentateuchal Laws, which represent these ideas and taboos, is new, and it compels a new attitude towards the question of the observance or the violation of these laws. . . .

The Liberal Jew holds his services on Sunday, and part of them, at least, in the vernacular languages, and so thorough is the attempt to modernize, which means in effect to Westernize, the Jewish religion , that in the

synagogue of which he is a minister, Dr. Mattuck has
" incorporated one of the greatest Sonnets of Shakespeare into the most sacred of all the Services ". Dis-
regarding tradition and the always powerful call of the
blood, there is, it seems to me, from the point of view
of religion, a far greater and more essential difference
between the Chief Rabbi and Mr. Montefiore than exists
between Mr. Montefiore and the great bulk of modern
English Protestant Nonconformists.

Mr. Montefiore insists over and over again that the
Jewish religion is a universal religion. He and some of
his friends, though by no means all (the American
Rabbi Wise is a noted exception) have no sympathy
whatever with the re-establishment of Jewish Nationalism in Palestine. He holds paradoxically that " the
Jewish religion has made the Jewish state almost inconceivable ". The Jewish religion is the religion of the
Jews, but Mr. Montefiore does not believe that it is
narrowly racial in its inspiration, else he certainly would
not approve the recitation in the synagogue on the Day
of Atonement of a sonnet of Shakespeare.

It is not to Moses that the Liberal Jews look, but to
the great Prophets, Isaiah, Amos, and Hosea, the
noblest figures in the long-drawn-out history of the
People of Israel. Their ambition is to adapt their
own lives to the exalted ethical teaching of these great
Prophets. It is very clear from Mr. Montefiore's
writing that Liberal Judaism is a personal religion,
and that is exactly what the traditional Jewish religion
is not.

" Hebraism ", writes Mr. Leon Simon, in *Studies in*

Jewish Nationalism, " tends to insist on the Hebrew nation as the mediating term between its individual members and the Infinite, and for that reason the Hebrew, as individual, is relatively incapable of achieving in his own life the synthesis of spirit and body, of attaining complete harmony and equilibrium." Mr. Montefiore finds this complete harmony and equilibrium in Liberal Judaism, as Dean Inge finds it in Christian Modernism.

Liberal Judaism derives its converts partly from the Orthodox, but mainly, I believe, from the indifferent, from the large class of modern Jew, to whom the religion of his fathers has become little more than a memory, and to whom that religion has now been given significance by the sincere attempt to adapt it to the conditions of modern life. I am, however, doubtful whether Liberal Judaism can continue to exist except as a branch of a vaguely theistic ethical Church, calculated to attract the always small number of thoughtful persons who are fearful of sentiment and romance. Mr. Montefiore apparently believes that Unitarianism is certain to be the religion of the future. I do not, because mankind will remain sentimental and romantic.

Liberal Judaism is essentially a cold religion. Mr. Montefiore accepts the dictum of Maimonides that "the only attributes applicable to God are negative". The Liberal Jew rejects the belief that God has ever interfered with the normal course of natural events. " Liberal Judaism ", Mr. Montefiore says, " must live without miracles or it will not be able to live at all." The Rabbi Mattuck goes farther. He points out that in the centuries just before and after the beginning of the Christian era, when many proselytes were made by Jewish missionaries, " Jewish converts came mostly from the educated classes, while the first converts to Christianity came from the depressed classes ". Again he says: " Judaism can expect proselytes only from those who have an intellectual appreciation and understanding of religious thought," from, that is, the religious *intelligentsia* who nowadays attend the meetings of the Modern Churchman's Union. Mr. Montefiore does not profess to have any very definite knowledge of the nature of God, or to have that contact with the Eternal which Christianity claims to establish between the Creator and the creature. I have extracted the following passages from his writings:

" Just as God is the God of truth, and as the laws of nature are His laws, so is God goodness and love, as man is growingly able to discern them in increasing purity and fulness, are His laws—laws which, by His very nature, He must wish us to discover and to obey. If He helps us at all, He has helped and helps us in this discovery and obedience. Thus to sin against God is to sin against goodness: the one implies the other reciprocally, for to sin against goodness is to sin against God."

" The conquest of sin, whether sudden or gradual, is in either case the combined result of human endeavour and the divine grace. The particular features in it upon which Judaism has always laid the greatest stress are repentance and atonement."

" This only we hold: that no punishment can be other than remedial, disciplinal, or educational, and that therefore no punishment can be ' eternal '."

THE JEWISH RELIGION

" Judaism did not deny the life beyond death, it left that future life in the hands of God; the conception of an everlasting hell was tacitly or definitely abandoned, and men were bid to do their duty upon earth, and to leave the world to come to the justice and mercy of God. Under the influence of teachings such as these the average cultivated Jew in the nineteenth century tended, except at funerals, to think (I fancy) less than the average cultivated Christian about immortality and the life beyond the grave. The percentage of Western Jews in the nineteenth century who were troubled by any fear of hell or purgatory (both of them conceptions known to Judaism as well as to Christianity, though less prominent in Judaism) was probably a good deal lower than the percentage of Western Christians."

" The life, of the world to come is the life, of the world which is, and as the old Rabbis said of it, all Sabbath because there is nothing in it which is unhallowed or unsabbattical."

" The modern Jewish hope of immortality is sound and pure. The desire for reward has passed away. The essence of our belief in immortality is this: with all the imperfections, the evil, the agony, the horrors, which have ever existed among men, and which still exist to-day, immortality seems to us to be the inseparable corollary or *sequitur* to a belief in a ruling, a righteous and a loving God. To that belief we wistfully cling, because, hard as the world is to explain with God, harder still, as it seems to us, is it to explain the world without God. Into the character and nature of that immortality Jews enquire seldom and little; yet while they do not depreciate this life because of that other life, it is just as false to say that, at the expense of *that* life, they unduly magnify *this* life. Their position is, I think, best represented in a single sentence by that paradoxical saying of the old Rabbi (a great favourite of mine;

163

and quoted also by Leo Baeck in his chapter on Judaism in Clemen's book): 'Better than the whole life of the world to come is an hour of repentance and good deeds in *this* world; but better than all the life of this world is an hour of bliss in the world to come.' "

The Liberal Jew pays little regard to the ceremonial laws. I again quote Mr. Montefiore, who writes in his tract, "What Constitutes a Jew?":

> If you believe that God really told Moses that the Israelites were never to light a fire on Saturday, your abstention has a religious value: if you refrain simply as an outward bond, your ceremonial act becomes bereft of any religious meaning. For, in order to possess religious and spiritual worth, an outward act must be the expression of some faith, some belief, some strongly held principle. It must be an outward symbol of an inward truth. Or so far as the outward rites of the community are concerned, it must be in itself beautiful as well as historic, an act to seize the imagination and impress the mind. Or the act must help the doer of it to live well. But if it is done *merely* as a means of keeping a religious fellowship together, which, moreover, would appear to possess no definite and positive doctrines that make it worth while to *keep* it together—if it is done *merely* as a sort of mark of distinctiveness—it ceases to possess any religious significance.

His attitude to traditional ceremonial and traditional religious observances has again its exact parallel among Liberal Christians. Such an ecclesiastic as the Bishop of Croydon might well apply all that Mr. Montefiore says of the Mosaic Law to the Catholic practice of fasting Communion.

While there are obviously these many points of

similarity between Liberal Judaism and modern Protestantism, Mr. Montefiore is emphatic that the two
things are very different. He has even gone so far
as to say that if Judaism is true, Christianity is false.
The basic dogma of Orthodox Christianity is that Christ
was God Incarnate. The whole idea of the Incarnation
of God in man is, to all religious Jews, something
very like blasphemy, to the Liberal as well as to the
Orthodox. But it should be remembered that the
Christian Unitarian rejects the doctrine of the Incarnation, that, while the Unitarians are themselves a small
body, a considerable section of Congregationalists to-
day are practically Unitarian, and that the Incarnation
is held very vaguely by a still larger body of nominal
Christians who entirely reject the doctrine of the
Virgin Birth. So that when Mr. Montefiore says that
if Judaism is true, Christianity is false, he means to
say that if, on the one hand, Liberal Judaism and
Christian Modernism are true, then Orthodox Christianity is at least partially false.

This is no place for the discussion of theological
dogma, but it is necessary to point out that the
Christian assertion is that the intention of the Incarnation was the revelation of the Nature of the Deity to
man, and that all that man can ever know of the
character of the Infinite, he must learn from the earthly
life of Christ, who was God Incarnate in man. " No
man cometh unto the Father but by Me." Dr. Mattuck
says that it is easier to know Christ than to know God.
The Christian answer is that man cannot know God
except through knowing Christ.

To the outside observer the position of the Liberal Jew is a highly interesting and at the same time an extemely pathetic attempt to save a great inheritance by throwing overboard most of its essentials. For if the Jews, as a separate community, cannot continue to exist without the retention of active faith in the Jewish religion, so it seems that the Jewish religion has no chance of continuance in the modern world if the idea of Jewish nationality is totally abandoned, as it has been by Dr. Mattuck and Mr. Montefiore. Mr. Leon Simon says:

Judaism, robbed of its national basis, has no chance of life. Its ceremonial practices become irksome and apparently useless in a form of civilized life with which they have no essential connection. Its moral teachings are displaced by the English or French or German morality which the emancipated Jew unconsciously imbibes with his English or French or German education. And as a set of metaphysical dogmas it has little appeal to the modern man. For Judaism has no message of salvation for the individual soul, as Christianity has: all its ideas are bound up with the existence of the Jewish nation.

Hence those emancipated Jews who are most religiously minded in the modern sense, those who are most concerned with the salvation of their individual souls, tend to go over to Christianity, or to evolve a form of so-called Judaism which is only a stepping-stone to Christianity; and those who remain more or less true to traditional Judaism are just those whose cravings for individual salvation are least strong—so that with the outside world, for which spirituality means other-worldliness, the Jew gets the reputation of being a materialist. It is a strange sequel to the long history of a nation whose whole life has been a spiritual struggle, whose whole conception of nationality has for so long been bound up with the idea of the one God.

Take away the idea of the nation as the divinely ordained mediator between the individual and the Eternal, and the whole structure of the Jewish religion tumbles to pieces, for Judaism deprived of its intensely national emphasis, had nothing to offer the individual in the troubled circumstances of the modern world. I again quote from Mr. Leon Simon:

> The ordinary man has a pragmatic need of God for help and comfort in time of trouble: and the lady who (as recorded by William James) said that it was 'so nice to be able to cuddle up to God' was giving naïve expression to a fundamental truth about religion. But Hebraism revolts from any humanisation of God, and its God is relatively of little use for cuddling purposes.

The ambition of Liberal Judaism is to attract back to an up-to-date fold the thousands who have lapsed from their religion. Among Christians to-day the wealthy and the intellectuals are largely pagan, and the poor, except where they have been influenced by the Catholic religion, are either entirely indifferent or openly hostile to religion. The majority of practising Christians belong to the middle-class in its various strata. Among the Jews it is the poor, the oppressed, and the persecuted who cling most steadfastly to the ancient faith. The walls of the ghetto were the protection of the Jewish religion as well as of the Jewish dream

of a restored nation. In England it is the poor Jews
of Whitechapel who find most consolation in the
promises of the God of Israel, and who are most
meticulous in their fulfilment of ceremonial laws and
religious obligations. As the Jew in the Western world
grows richer and becomes more assimilated, he
generally becomes as un-religious as his Christian
neighbours. He may go to the synagogue on the Day
of Atonement as the Christian next door may go to
church on Easter Day, but religion plays no vital
part in his life.

The pious Jew and the Jew, convinced that it is
only the Jewish religion that can preserve the Jewish
race, admit and deplore the decadence of Orthodox
observances. In July of this year, the *Jewish Chronicle*
published a remarkable article on " The Oxford
Movement and Ourselves ", in which, after referring
to the influence of Keble and Pusey on the life of the
Church of England, the writer went on to say:

> The story may well give English Jews something to think
> about. The Synagogue is in the grip of decay. Our own
> religious centres present an air of dull acquiescence and
> perfunctory routine. There is no inspiration. It is the day
> of small things and, despite a stirring here and a move-
> ment there, the masses slip away in increasing numbers,
> and our religious leaders seem to lack the power to call
> the wanderers back. Week after week, the cries go up of
> Religion Classes in financial distress, but however mourn-
> ful and even piercing, they awaken only a poor response.
> And our workers and leaders go plodding along their
> several paths, sunk in the rut of deficits and appeals,
> pleased with such extensions of their work as they may

effect, but only half-conscious, seemingly, of the wide-spread conditions and tendencies that will sooner or later, and with dead inevitability, bring their labours to nought. How many congregants, I wonder, are likely to be found, fifty years hence, in the synagogues which the United Synagogue is busily building in outer London? How many, I repeat—with thousands of Jewish children growing up around it devoid of religious teaching? There is a fatuousness about it all which must strike alarm into the sturdiest hearts! . . . .

One could go on cataloguing the activities of the latter-day children of the Oxford Movement, but *cui bono*? They spring from a great impulse, and that impulse our Community seems incapable of imparting. It might be given if our ablest and most earnest men and women would be content to forget their societies for a little and come together to think, to survey the broad situation, to invite large ideas from thinkers. In such an assemblage some new inspiration might be struck, and in its counsels, enriched by imagination and stimulated by well-grounded anxieties, who knows but that some day a Jewish leader might be born with the poetry and pathos and eloquence and magnetism of the great Dr. Newman himself, of whom Gladstone wrote that "without ostentation or effort but by simple excellence, he was continually drawing undergraduates more and more around him"? I believe that prophecy is not dead in Israel, and I would not admit that a prophet may not arise one day even on the seemingly sterile soil of English Jewry. On the contrary, I meet, every week, young men and women, of idealism and vision and earnestness, longing to speak and to do, but there is no direction, no movement by whose stimulus they would be swept up into a great revivalist effort and give to it, in return, their own enthusiasm and inspiration.

Let us begin by getting together and taking our bearings, and let us get hold of the truth that what matters to-day

169

is not so much minor differences as the widespread indifference and hostility to any religion at all. Even in America the barriers between Orthodoxy and Reform are crumbling, and they are falling here, too, if only we had the courage to admit it. Orthodox and Reformers have something better to do than to proclaim their incompatibilities. They have materialism to fight, and a message to evolve for many of our young, which will take note alike of their longings and perplexities, and bring them to the service of their people and their faith.

The German persecutions have revived " dormant Jewish consciousness". Jews, like the writer of this article are convinced that Israel can only be saved by the God of Israel. But " the dormant Jewish consciousness " is still only half awake. The Jew, with the rest of the world, is vastly affected by the world-wide irreligion. The good Jew is also the good Englishman, the good Frenchman, and the good American, with a thousand interests and pre-occupations. And judging from their literature, it is as difficult for Orthodox and Liberals to co-operate in the fight against unbelief as it is for Roman Catholics and Methodists.

As it seems to me, Orthodox Judaism is a religion more calculated to respond effectively to genuine human needs than the Liberalism which has derived from it. " Our primal duty is faith in the God of Israel and in His servant Moses," said Dr. Hertz, the Chief Rabbi, in a recent sermon. This is the great monotheistic expression of faith to which the Moslem " Allah is Allah and Mohamed is His Prophet ", is the complement. " Judaism ", says the Chief Rabbi,

THE JEWISH RELIGION

" is a religious civilisation, a spiritual culture, aglow with a passion for righteousness. It has its own national language, literature, history, customs and social institutions." Its law is the Law of the Torah, set out in the five books of Moses and elaborated into what is known as the Oral Law, which consists of an immense series of commentaries, written by Rabbis and Doctors throughout the centuries. The Jewish creed is set out in the Thirteen Principles of the Faith (of which Mr. Montefiore says he disbelieves in five or six), drawn up by Maimonides and printed in the Jewish Prayer Book :

1. I believe with perfect faith that the Creator, blessed be his name, is the Author and Guide of everything that has been created, and that he alone has made, does make, and will make all things.

2. I believe with perfect faith that the Creator, blessed be his name, is a Unity, and that there is no unity in any manner like unto his, and that he alone is our God, who was, is, and will be.

3. I believe with perfect faith that the Creator, blessed be his name, is not a body, and that he is free from all the accidents of matter, and that he has not any form whatsoever.

4. I believe with perfect faith that the Creator, blessed be his name, is the first and the last.

5. I believe with perfect faith that to the Creator, blessed be his name, and to him alone, it is right to pray, and that it is not right to pray to any being besides him.

6. I believe with perfect faith that all the words of the prophets are true.

7. I believe with perfect faith that the prophecy of Moses our teacher, peace be unto him, was true, and that

171

he was the chief of the prophets, both of those that preceded and of those that followed him.

8. I believe with perfect faith that the whole Law, now in our possession, is the same that was given to Moses our teacher, peace be unto him.

9. I believe with perfect faith that this Law will not be changed, and that there will never be any other law from the Creator, blessed be his name.

10. I believe with perfect faith that the Creator, blessed be his name, knows every deed of the children of men, and all their thoughts, as it is said, It is he that fashioneth the hearts of them all, that giveth heed to all their deeds.

11. I believe with perfect faith that the Creator, blessed be his name, rewards those that keep his commandments, and punishes those that transgress them.

12. I believe with perfect faith in the coming of the Messiah, and, though he tarry, I will wait daily for his coming.

13. I believe with perfect faith that there will be a resurrection of the dead at the time when it shall please the Creator, blessed be his name, and exalted be the remembrance of him for ever and ever.

For thy salvation I hope, O Lord! I hope, O Lord, for thy salvation! O Lord, for thy salvation, I hope!

The ceremonial laws, the regulations concerning food and so on, are by no means merely materialistic. They have indeed a genuine spiritual significance. The Chief Rabbi has said:

The aim and purpose of the multitudinous laws and regulations of the Oral Law are nothing less than the hallowing influence of religion; in brief, the sanctification of human life. Religious observance, historic commemoration, sacred precept, and hallowed custom keep ever before the Israelite the thought of consecration.

THE JEWISH RELIGION

Orthodox Judaism is much more definitely anti-Christian than Liberal Judaism, and it is unquestionably true that the divergence in religious belief, so long as it continues, not only ensures the separatism that the Orthodox Jew desires, but will remain the cause of dislike, suspicion, and occasional persecution. It is, I fear, a fact that must be accepted, that if the Jew is to continue a Jew, he must live with the possibility of dislike, distraint, and misrepresentation.

The Orthodox Jew is fearful even of expressing any sort of admiration for the character of Christ. He occasionally allows himself to speak of Him in terms that are peculiarly offensive to Christian people. Stephen Wise, the famous Liberal Jewish Rabbi, has often expressed great admiration for Christ and has been denounced on the grounds that such admiration " leads to Baptism ". In view of the long experience of persecution, all this seems to me easy to understand, even though it is certainly to be deplored.

The Jewish religion as a vital force in the lives of millions of people is steadily decreasing, and it is possible that its influence and its faith are fated to become a tiny cult. If it does, a very noble thing will have passed away. Judaism is the religion of a nation, but it is also the religion of the family. The observance of the Sabbath, and its fine significance and its social importance, begins with the meeting of the family on the Friday night, and one protection of the social institution on which civilization has gradually been built, will be lost if Judaism disappears.

THE JEW TO-DAY

It is threatened to-day on the one hand by the assimilation of the successful and the intellectual Jews, not into Christianity, but into the neo-pagan society which includes so many nominal Christians, and on the other hand, by the anti-religious propaganda of the Communists which is everywhere attracting many thousands of young Jews of the working and small trading classes.

CHAPTER 6

JEWISH CULTURE

THE noblest aspect of Zionism is its ambition to pre-serve and develop Jewish culture. With this ambition the Hebrew university was founded in Jerusalem to be the home of what Renan called *l'esprit sémitique*. All genuine distinctive cultures are eminently worth preserving. But with other phrases which I have already examined, *l'esprit sémitique*, as it exists in the Western world, is illusory and almost impossible to discover and define. " One does not need to have the authentic Hittite nose to be a Jew," writes Houston Chamberlain in *The Foundations of the Nineteenth Century*, "the term Jew rather denotes a special way of thinking and feeling." What is this special way?

The Jews far more than the Greeks are the fathers of European culture. To western Europe the Jews have given the most beautiful of its nursery stories, four-fifths of its most suggestive imagery, a large part of its inspiration to courage—who can forget David and Goliath?—to patience, to sane judgment, and to faith. Protestant Christianity at its best is predomin-antly Jewish, and it is now established that Catholic sacramentalism derives from Judaism, and only in a

very limited degree from the Greek mystery religions.
The American, H. L. Mencken, says:

> These same Jews, from time immemorial, have been
> the chief dreamers of the human race, and beyond all com-
> parison its greatest poets. It was Jews who wrote the
> magnificent poems called the Psalms, the Song of Solomon,
> and the Books of Job and Ruth; it was Jews who gave
> us the Beatitudes, the Sermon on the Mount, the incom-
> parable ballad of the Christ Child, and the twelfth of
> Romans. I incline to believe that the scene recounted in
> John viii, 3–11, is the most poignant drama ever written
> in the world, as the Song of Solomon is unquestionably
> the most moving love song, and the Twenty-third Psalm
> the greatest of hymns. All these transcendent riches
> Christianity inherits from a little tribe of sedentary
> Bedouins, so obscure and unimportant that secular history
> scarcely knows them. No heritage of modern man is
> richer and none has made a more brilliant mark upon
> human thought, not even the legacy of the Greeks.

" The Jews ", said Wagner, " have never had an
art of their own." That is untrue. The art of the Old
Testament is stupendous.

But the Jews have given their ancient treasures to
the world! They are no more exclusively theirs. The
Psalms of David are chanted every day in the Divine
Office in Catholic churches. Joseph, Moses, David,
Daniel are world heroes. The great Hebrew prophets
are the cherished assets of the Christian Church. The
Sacred Books of the East are sacred only to the East.
The Koran is to Europeans a literary curiosity. But
the Hebrew Scriptures are a vital part of the Christian
Bible. The Catholic Church was not a new creation

but, as its adherents believe, the perfection of the Jewish Church as it existed before the birth of Christ. Ancient Jewish culture, therefore, remains the most priceless possession of humanity. Is there a modern Jewish culture? Having given to his fellows so much, has the Jew retained some distinctive imaginative and cultural possessions that have remained exclusively his own?

It is the Zionist dream that modern Jewish culture shall be maintained in Jerusalem and in its Hebrew university. But, in all the circumstances, there is considerable justification for the suggestion that the actual aim is to create and not to preserve. "I have not used the dubious word 'culture'," says Mr. Montefiore in one of his essays, "but it might be said that Jewish culture is the spirit of the Jewish religion." In so far, then, as the modern Jew has abandoned his religion, he has lost his peculiar culture, for, as Mr. Christopher Dawson says, "every culturally vital society must possess a religion". To the Zionist Jewish culture is national and not religious, but there is really no such thing as a national culture. And Mr. Montefiore says: "It is really nationalism which is being put forward in a religious disguise. The Jews as a nation are to develop a national culture."

Certainly to-day there is no definite and distinctive Jewish culture as there are a definite and distinctive Catholic culture, a definite and distinctive Protestant culture, the new definite and distinctive Bolshevist culture, and at least the remnants of a definite and distinctive Chinese culture. Literally and absolutely

the Jew has given himself away—the best of himself.
Within the ghetto, a Hebrew culture was preserved,
and a Hebrew and Yiddish literature, inspired by the
Bible and the Talmud, was produced, a trickling
stream almost poignant in its inferiority to its great
derivative river. But the Jew in the modern world,
with whom I am concerned, has escaped from the
ghetto. He is a European living among Europeans.
When he is a great thinker, he is a European thinker.
When he is a great poet, he no longer sings the songs
of Zion.

My friend the Rev. A. E. Baker (and no man is
better equipped for the job), has been good enough
to write for insertion in this chapter an analysis of
the great modern Jewish thinkers, beginning with
Spinoza and ending with Einstein. Mr. Baker says:

" Jewish philosophical thought in Europe, even
before the general emancipation of the Jews, was
deeply influenced by the Gentile civilization which
surrounded it. In its turn it made a contribution of
inestimable value to general culture. A crucial illustration of this is Spinoza. He is recognized as at once
the greatest Jew since the New Testament, and one
of the greatest, some would say the greatest, of all
modern European philosophers. His life and character
were so transparently beautiful that the ' free thinkers '
of the eighteenth century used his name to illustrate
their contention that orthodoxy is not a necessary condition of the good life. He was excommunicated by
the local Amsterdam synagogue in his early manhood;

during all his working life he was separated from his people. But the Jews now claim him as one of the great ornaments of Jewry. The forces that made him, however, are known. And it can be said that it is impossible to disentangle among them the Jewish from the non-Jewish. The two elements mingle and separate and mix again.

" The story of the influence of Spinoza on the thought of the world since his day has been the subject of minutely detailed research. It is a very impressive influence, in its variety and depth as well as in its extent. He did much to mould the minds of the greatest writers of all, and, increasingly as time went on, of men and women of all kinds. But the tale of the effect of Spinoza on modern thought contains relatively few Jewish names, even when told by an enthusiastic Jew like Mr. Leon Roth, the Professor of Philosophy in the University of Jerusalem, and the author of an admirable book on Spinoza.[1]

" The philosophy of Spinoza is a hymn to unity. His argument begins with God and never leaves Him. He sees all minds, all things in Him. In God the obstinate dualism is overcome of mind and space, of spirit and matter. It was Novalis who first called him the God-intoxicated man. Some see the authentic Jewish tradition here. There is no argument about the existence of God in the Bible, because there is no doubt of Him and His power. But it is equally true that in this aspect of his teaching Spinoza is the heir of the Platonist tradition in European philosophy. Aris-

[1] *Spinoza*, by Leon Roth. (Benn, 1929.)

totelianism derived general ideas from the particulars of experience, and made God the conclusion of an argument. On the other hand, experience merely reminded the neo-Platonist of the highest certainties. He believed that the mind knows God directly. That is Spinoza's position. The very possibility of a true statement at all on any subject involves, for him, the being of God; for all thinking is really thinking about God.

" There is no more moving picture in the whole history of philosophy than that of this noble Jew, descendant of Marranos (Jews persecuted into outward conformity with Catholicism), himself excommunicated from the synagogue, living remote, solitary, with nothing but the barest minimum of physical necessities, but calmly happy, fighting a losing battle with phthisis, dying at the age of forty-four, with his thoughts and desires dissociated from the trivialities of temporal things and attached to that which is eternal.

" Spinoza's attitude to Christianity has been described by the Archbishop of York:[1]

' If it must be said that Spinoza was not a Christian because he did not accept a specific historic revelation, it is only at that point that this compatriot of the historic Christ falls short of full discipleship. With Plato he fails to rise to belief in self-sacrifice as a quality of the Supreme —and for the same reason. But he believed with all his heart in the eternal wisdom of God which has revealed itself in all things, especially in the human mind, and most of all in Jesus Christ.'

" As a thinker, Spinoza was a citizen of the world. His mind, doubtless, was moulded by the Bible and

[1] *Christianity and the State*, by W. Temple, pp. 20, 21.

the medieval Jewish thinkers. But the contents of that
mind were supplied by non-Jews. Descartes represents
to him the new knowledge. The naturalistic politics
which he did so much to teach the world he derived
from Hobbes. From Bacon he learned the importance
of experiment. The scholastic logic came to him
through many contemporary writers. Mr. Roth sums
it up: ' He took what he could whence he could, yet
he adhered to his original vision.'[1]

" The widespread, deep, and increasing influence of
Spinoza may be symbolized by the aphorism of
Hegel, that to become a philosopher a student must
first soak himself in Spinoza, and by the judgment of
the Archbishop of York that he is the one modern
philosopher who is worthy to be named in the same
breath with Plato. Bishop Berkeley read him. He is
the father of scientific Biblical criticism, a science
largely confined to Gentiles. Leibnitz deliberately con-
cealed his great obligation to Spinoza. Through
Solomon Maimon he influenced the development of
Kant. Lessing said that his was the only true philosophy. Goethe studied him earnestly at three difficult
periods of his life. Fichte was profoundly affected by
him. Shelling was an avowed Spinozist, and Hegel
used the central ideas of Spinoza as the foundations
of his own system. And in all the list there is only one
Jewish name ! It has been said that ' when we say
that the Jews gave us Spinoza this is literally true, as
they did not want him themselves '.[2]

[1] *Op. cit.*, p. 235.
[2] *Moses Mendelssohn*, by H. Walters, p. 19.

" The next great Jewish name in modern specula-
tion is that of Karl Marx. There was practically no
religion of any kind in Marx's upbringing. His father
was strongly imbued with eighteenth century ideas,
and, when Karl was six years old he became legally,
though only nominally, a Protestant. Karl Marx was
a scholar of wide, though not exact reading, but he
was not a profound or very original thinker. Lenin
says, truly enough, that he continued and completed
the three chief ideological currents of the early nineteenth century, represented respectively by the three
most advanced countries of the human race: classical
German philosophy, classical English political econ-
omy, and French socialism combined with French
revolutionary doctrines.[1] It does not need to be said
that there is nothing particularly Jewish in any of
these currents of thought.

" Marx was a materialist. He believed that this life
is all there is. He did not believe in God as the ground
of the universe or as the cause of any event in it; and
he did not believe in prayer as the means towards the
solution of any problem, practical or theoretical. He
disliked and opposed Christianity because those who
profit by the present commercial and industrial system
—capitalists and those dependent on them—supported
and were supported by official religion. His well-known
phrase that ' religion is the opium of the people '[2] means
that it causes men and women to acquiesce in evil condi-

---

[1] *The Teaching of Karl Marx*, by V. I. Lenin, p. 11. Reprinted from Vol.
xviii of *The Collected Works of Lenin*.

[2] *Essay on* Hegel's *Philosophy of Law*, by Marx.

tions. ' The social principles of Christianity preach cowardice, self-contempt, abasement, submission, humility . . . but the proletariat, which will not allow itself to be treated as canaille, regards its courage, self-confidence, independence, and sense of personal dignity as more necessary than its daily bread '.[1]

" Marx had no contacts with Judaism whatever, and owed nothing to the Bible or to any Jewish book. Hyndman, who had a soft, romantic attitude to life and men, thought that he saw in Marx a combination of ' the righteous fury of the great prophets of his race ' and ' the cold analytical powers of Spinoza and the Jewish doctors '. But if there were anything in that it would mean that all disinterestedness derives from Spinoza and that there is no ethical passion in the world but that of the Hebrew prophets.

" Marx insists that his is a dialectic materialism. That expresses his debt to Hegel, and it is an attempt to make materialism the philosophy of evolution and history and above all, of revolution. Hegelianism describes nature and history as developing through a serious of conflicts of opposing principles, followed in each case by a synthesis of what has been opposed. Hegel recognized contradiction as the dynamic of the cosmic and historical process. ' Contradiction,' he says, ' is what actually moves the world.' Any idea or notion, as the mind contemplates it, is seen to imply and lead to its opposite; and there is contradiction and disharmony until a more comprehensive and concrete conception is found, in the richer content of which

[1] *Gesamtausgabe*, by Marx, Abt. I, Bd. 6, p. 278.

183

is included and reconciled all that is true in each of the contradictory, more abstract, notions. Marx thought that he saw the same process going on in the life of society. Any economic system actually existing, any form of social organization, because it over-stresses one-sidedly an aspect of human life which is never quite complete and adequate, leads to a reaction, a revolt, a violently contradictory process of thinking, a type of social and economic life at the other extreme from what has been.

" There is nothing specifically Jewish in Marx's thought. Many Jews have been poor and disinherited, from the days when they sat down and wept beside the waters of Babylon! But that does not make resentment against injustice particularly Jewish. There is an apocalyptic note in Marx. He looked for a cata-clysmic disappearance of the present world-order, a sudden coming of the Kingdom of Man, which is reminiscent of the expectations of some Jewish heretics at the beginning of the Christian era. But Berdiaeff has recognized that apocalyptic hope as characteristic-ally Russian; and he should know, for he is a Russian himself, and an ex-Marxian. But however that may be, it is enough to show that it cannot be pressed as characteristically Jewish.

" The next great Jewish name in the history of European thought is Henri Louis Bergson. Born in 1859, he was influenced by Latin and Greek authors, particularly Zeno with his puzzle about Achilles and the tortoise; by mathematics; by the science of Darwin. His philosophy is largely a reaction against

Herbert Spencer's mechanistic materialism, and the undogmatic scepticism of Taine and Renan. But no one could have been more completely unaffected by Jewish thought than was Bergson.

" The fundamental intuition of Bergson's philosophy is the reality of time. This, he holds, means freedom, novelty, creation, and some kind of belief in some kind of God. At the end of the nineteenth century he restored to men who had been brought up on materialism and the denial of truth, the feeling of the presence of God. The paradox is this, that while more than one of the best known of the French intellectuals have attributed to him their conversion to Catholicism, three of his books have been put on the *Index*. This is probably to be explained by his excessive and exclusive emphasis on the Immanence of God—a tendency which he shares with Spinoza, although it is as far as can be from orthodox Judaism.

" Bergson's philosophy is an interpretation of evolution. If there has been a real development, so that the end is not only more complicated, but richer, more interesting, more valuable, than the beginning, then evolution cannot be explained on mechanical principles. The mere rearrangement of atoms or molecules present at the beginning can yield nothing really 'new'. True evolution means that time is real, that it makes a difference; it is a qualitative *durée* which we live and experience, much more than a mere quantity which can be symbolized by a line or any other spatial concept. It means that determination is invalid. There is genuine novelty in life and history, 'a ceaseless

upspringing of something new '. There is more in to-day
than yesterday can explain. Freewill is a factor in the
real world, and the mind's independence of the body.
Bergson thinks that he has proved that the mind is
related to the brain and body as a pianist is related
to a piano.

" The other aspect of evolution to which Bergson
has called attention is its discontinuity. A new species
is evolved, not by an indefinite number of minute
changes, but by a smaller number of ' jumps ' or
measurable changes. The Life Force, the Creative
Power, is ever making new experiments. Evolution is
the record of one comparative failure after another.
But the Life Force tries ever new ways to accomplish
similar ends. It expresses itself ever more adequately.
Bergson leaves an impression of boundless creativity,
infinite resourcefulness, freedom, and irrepressible
novelty.

" In his great monograph on *The Two Sources of
Religion and Morality*, Bergson devotes only one short
paragraph to Judaism. He points out that Christianity
meant a profound transformation of Judaism. ' For
a religion which was essentially national was substi-
tuted a religion capable of becoming universal.' To
a God of justice, whose justice was the affair of his
subjects, succeeded a God of Love, who loved all the
world. ' Jehovah was too severe a judge; between
Israel and her God there was not enough intimacy for
Judaism to become a mysticism in the sense we have
defined.' But he goes on to claim, quite rightly, that
it was because the prophets had a passion for

righteousness that Christian mysticism, when it came, was able to pass beyond mere contemplation to an active mysticism, capable of conquering the world.

" Another distinguished Jewish philosopher, happily still with us, is Dr. Samuel Alexander, an Australian who is Emeritus-Professor of Philosophy in the University of Manchester. Like Bergson, he was born in 1859. His philosophy is in many ways vastly different from that of Bergson, but they are both systems of realism, and each of them can be considered as an interpretation of evolution.

" The mere outgrowth of life from matter and of mind from life, suggests a further quality of existence beyond mind, which is related to mind as mind is related to life or life to matter. That quality Alexander calls deity, and the being which possesses it is God. The world is a world striving or tending to deity; it has in this sense a divine character. Deity has not in its distinctive nature as yet emerged at this stage of the world's existence. God is a being whose body is the world of nature, but that world conceived as actually possessing deity, and therefore he is not actual as an existent but only as an ideal, and only existent in so far as the tendency towards his distinctive character is existent in the actual world.[1]

" Alexander has himself suggested some objections which may be raised to his account of religion. Perhaps they may be summed up in the statement that no religion which exists, or ever has existed, would accept this explanation of the words deity and God.

[1] Alexander, in *Science and Religion: A Symposium*. (Howe) p. 136.

God, as he can be known by men and women, according to Alexander, does not yet exist. Perhaps he never will exist. Indeed, there is a real sense in which it is true to say that for Alexander God never will exist, for deity is like to-morrow, it is always to come but never comes. Deity will always be the name of the next quality which is to emerge but has not yet emerged, something which the eye hath not seen nor ear heard and which it has not entered man's heart to imagine. In no sense is Alexander's God the Creator; indeed, he is created. We create him by our striving. And only in a very attenuated sense of the word is he transcendent. Worship, as humanity has understood it, is explained away. For not even a philosopher can worship the non-existent. It is significant, perhaps, that Dr. Alexander has admitted that it is only occasionally that he has the religious feeling. There is nothing from the beginning to the end of his important book which shows any obligation, direct or indirect, to Judaism. It is essentially an atheistic naturalism. It explains the higher by the lower, and offers a definite contradiction to the first words of Genesis.

" One of the best known of living Jews is Sigmund Freud. His writings have had an enormous influence, direct and indirect, all over the world. He is by training a doctor of medicine, and he has specialized in mental disease. On the basis of a particular speculative theory of what the human mind is and how it works, he has built up an elaborate method of healing known as psycho-analysis. Many patients have been cured by this method. A very great number indeed have not improved under the treatment. Allers says that so far as his experience goes there is no case of neurosis that inevitably necessitates psycho-analysis. And Sir Robert Armstrong-Jones, an alienist of European reputation, says that he has seen several instances where people have, through psycho-analytical methods, been precipitated into the ranks of the certified insane in mental hospitals. In fact, the world could well dispense with this method altogether.

" Freud has also applied his theory of the mind to explain and co-ordinate art, literature, economics, religion, and indeed the whole of life and history. Psycho-analysis is no longer primarily a method of dealing with neurotics, or a particular kind of abnormal or normal psychology. It is a philosophy of life.. But it is safe to say that there is nothing in it which is characteristically Jewish.

" The writings of Freud and Jung and their followers are ' soaked and sodden in sex '. Every dream, every religious symbol, every more or less conscious physical habit, the interest which makes one boy collect stamps and another collect moths: all these express sexual interest or maladjustments.

" Religion is to be explained as a projection of one's feelings for one's father on to the sky, so to speak. A child thinks of its father with mingled love and terror. Man is a child who never grows up. Religion is only an externalization of the ' Father Image '. All that one thinks of, and expects, from God, is to be explained in that way. And the Œdipus Complex will explain why the dying God, the Crucified Saviour, plays so large a part in religion. Religion is an illusion; it expresses our unconscious wishes. It is the universal obsessional neurosis of humanity. It is religious education which is responsible for the rapid mental degeneration by which the radiant intelligence of the child becomes the feeble mentality of the average adult. The only hope for an intelligent race, in whom reason is strong enough to control impulse (we have forgotten now that ' mental processes are essentially unconscious ') lies in the experiment of a non-religious education.'

" Another living Jew, whose world-wide fame is perhaps as great as that of Freud, whose mental power is greater than his, whose influence will be more permanent, is Albert Einstein. The mathematical invention and discovery which have made possible the special and general theories of Relativity, and the view of the physical universe which goes with them, owe a good deal, also, to the work of Michelson, Minkowski, Weyl, and other brilliant Jews, as well as to Einstein. But no one will claim that there is a specially Jewish mathematics, or that its recent developments belong to any particular race.

" In 1887, Michelson and Morley, a Jew and a Gentile who, perhaps, did not realize that there was any such difference between them, performed a famous experiment with a beam of light which seemed to them to prove that if the earth is moving, the surrounding ether is moving with it. This was an important step towards the notion that there is no

---

¹ *The Future of an Illusion*, by Freud (*passim*).

absolute motion in the universe, and that all motion is merely relative.[1]

" In 1905 Einstein pointed out that absolute space and absolute time are figments of the imagination. The only space and time we can observe and measure are relative to certain standards of measurement—a unit of length, our pulse, the tick of a clock, and so on. Time and space are relative to the observer.[2] Einstein stated his Special Theory of Relativity in the words, ' If, relative to S.S' is a system moving with uniform velocity of translation, then natural phenomena run their course with respect to S' according to exactly the same general laws as with respect to S."[3] Eddington has shown that this is another way of saying that it is impossible by any experiment to detect uniform motion relative to the ether.[4]

" It was another Jew, Minkowski, who in 1908 pointed out that although space and time, taken separately, are relative to the observer, depending on his position and the direction and speed of his movements, the changes in space and time compensate each other, so that a combination of the two is the same for all observers. Minkowski says that time is a fourth dimension, one second corresponding to the 186,000 miles which light travels in that time. (That looks as though it means something, but it does not. It is one of the Moonbeams from the Larger Lunacy!) ' In the new continuum of space-time two events may

1 *The History of Science*, by Dampier-Whetham, pp. 417, 418.
2 Ibidem, p. 420.
3 A. Einstein: " *Relativity, The Special and the General Theory* ", p. 20.
4 *Space, Time, and Gravitation*, (Eddington) p. 20.

be said to be separated by an "interval", involving both space and time, which has a true absolute value whoever measures it." Herman Weyl, another clever Jew, has pointed out how difficult it is to imagine the relations between past and future in a world in which time is one dimension of a four-dimensional space-time continuum. ' The scene of action of reality is not a three-dimensional Euclidean space but rather a four-dimensional world in which space and time are linked together indissolubly. However deep the chasm may be that separates the intuitive nature of space from that of time in our experience, nothing of this qualitative difference enters into the objective world which physics endeavours to crystallize out of direct experience. It is a four-dimensional continuum, which is neither time nor space. Only the consciousness that passes on in one portion of this world experiences the detached piece which comes to meet it and passes behind it, as *history*, that is, as a process that is going forward in time and takes place in space.'

" It is impossible within my limits to attempt to discuss all the theoretical results of Relativity, and of the view of the universe as four-dimensional which goes with it. But one difficult simplification must be mentioned. If neither space nor time is absolute nor real, then the conception of matter as a substance extended in space and enduring in time must be abandoned. Matter must now be imagined as a series of events. And no one knows how one event is con-

---

[1] Dampier-Whetham, *op. cit.*, p. 422.
[2] H. Weyl, *Space–Time–Matter*, p. 217. Quoted by E. W. Barnes, *Scientific Theory and Religion*, p. 122.

nected with its successor. Gravitation, as a force, is
no longer necessary, for it is described by the Rela-
tivists as a curvature in space-time. In 1919, also,
Einstein invented a new Unitary Field Theory which
makes electro-magnetism, as well as gravity, a metric
property of space-time. The whole field of Physics
has now been reduced to one set of equations. In one
sense, the universe is described more simply than ever
before. The difficulty is that Einstein himself has said
that only one other living man understands relativity.
He is Emile Meyerson, a Pole by birth and a Frenchman by naturalization, the distinguished author of
several books on the philosophy of science, the influence of which is to been seen in more than one
modern book; for example, in Professor A. E.
Tayor's Gifford Lectures. And Meyerson also is a
Jew!

"Ludwig Borne once complained that some people
disliked him because he was a Jew, others tolerated
him in spite of his being a Jew, and yet others liked
him just because of his being a Jew, but nobody ever
forgot that he was a Jew. The story I have told
began with Spinoza and ended with Einstein. It includes thinkers so widely different as Marx and Alexander, as Bergson and Freud. Each in his own way,
these men have all made important contributions to
the one common culture which all Europeans—nay,
which all modern civilized people—share. They share
no common Jewish outlook. If we are to include
these so widely different minds in any unity, it can be
nothing narrower than our common humanity itself.

It would not be at all difficult to forget that they are Jews.''

I add a footnote to Mr. Baker's analysis. In their interesting book *The German Jew*, after summarizing the eminent work in medicine of German-Jewish doctors, the authors, Mr. Abraham Myerson and Isaac Goldberg, say (pp. 42, 43):

> Perhaps there has lived no group of men more characterized by candour, honesty, and selfless devotion to science than Cohn, Cohnheim, Weigert, and Ehrlich. In this, however, they were not in the least unlike their great German colleagues Virchow, Muller, and Koch. In fact, Virchow, at the height of the anti-Semitic fever of the 1880's, valiantly defended the Jews of his day. How could he as an honest man do otherwise? They were his colleagues, his pupils, and his collaborators.

Exactly. In the world of medicine '' there is neither Greek nor Jew, circumcision nor uncircumcision, Barbarian, Scythian, bond nor free ''.

I turn from philosophy and science to literature. While, as I have said, culture is never entirely national, workaday England, with its magnificent qualities of heart, and its limited powers of head, may be said to live and move and have its being in the pages of the Dickens novels. Dickens is England. Similarly, the most persistent qualities of the French are to be discovered in the writings of the ironists from Voltaire to Anatole France. But it is quite impossible to hear the distinctive voice of Jewry in her one great modern poet, Heinrich Heine, who, whether Nazi Germany likes it or not, will always live in the

history of literature as the greatest German poet since
Goethe. In his brilliant book *Dreamers of the Ghetto*,
the late Israel Zangwill makes Heine describe himself as "a German Parisian, a Jewish German, a
hated political exile who yearns for dear homely old
Germany, a sceptical sufferer with a Christian
patience, a romantic poet expressing in classical form
the modern spirit".

Heine is said by the pan-Aryan German to be
without those qualities of simplicity and piety which
the German, with small justification, loves to claim
for himself. But critical opinion remains in agreement
with Matthew Arnold that in Heine's poetry there is
the blending of "French modernism and clearness
with German sentiment and fulness". Technically
his poetry is entirely in the German tradition, since
he uses, I again quote Matthew Arnold, "a form of
old German popular poetry, a ballad form which has
more rapidity and grace than any ballad form of
ours". Arnold says that Heine had in him "both
the spirit of Greece and the spirit of Judæa". This is
attractive rhetoric, but it is little more. He had inherited from Goethe his profound admiration for
classic Greece and he was a Jew by descent, but as
Mr. Walter insists in his *Heinrich Heine: A Critical
Examination of the Poet and His Work*, he is certainly not a Jewish poet. "We experience no difficulty", says Mr. Walter, "in determining the ever
present French elements in the poetry of Victor Hugo
and Alfred de Musset, or the German element in
Goethe. But where are the Jewish elements in Heine's

poetry?" There is less Oriental colouring in it than in the poetry of Victor Hugo. His language is "chaste and simple rather than exuberant", and, Mr. Walter goes on:

> With the exception of a few excursions into Oriental imagery, his language is German to the core, and so are, on the whole, his feelings. If we find him, and that very rarely, in what appears to be a Jewish mood, as in the magnificent *Brich aus in lauten Klagen*, we must remember that Heine is also the author of the Catholic *Wallfahrt nach Kevlaar* and the intrinsically Christian poem entitled *Friede*, of the *Nordseebilder*. No mood was beyond his reach. The time when he first planned his *Rabbi von Bacharach* was probably the only period of his life when he evinced a desire to be considered a Jewish poet, and the failure of the work suggests that he may have discovered his own Jewish cultural background to be too thin to render his task possible. By the time he wrote:

> *Ich bin ein deutscher Dichter,*
> *Bekannt im deutschen Land;*
> *Nennt man die besten Namen,*
> *So wird auch der meine genannt;*

> he had realized that his poetry drew its best nourishment from the soil of European culture and that Occidental feeling and thought were the fundamental conditions of its development.

Heine was a rebel. His life was, as Matthew Arnold has said, "a life and death battle with Philistinism". He was the supreme flamboyant, always bashing away at the drab and always to his own suffering and discomfort. But the drab was represented for him by the Jew of the market-place as well as by the

Philistine who was not a Jew. With all other Jews, as with all other flamboyants, he had an intense admiration for Napoleon, since it was to Napoleon that the Jews of Middle Europe owed their small measure of political and intellectual liberty. He hated England because England was drab. He found a measure of Jewish pride in knowing that "since the Exodus, freedom was always spoken with a Hebrew accent". But his sense of race brought with it no spirit of exaltation. Mr. Israel Zangwill makes him say: "Judaism is not a religion but a misfortune, and to be born a Jew and a genius!—what a curse." Where in Heine's poetry is Renan's *l'esprit sémitique* to be found as *l'esprit français* can be found in Anatole France, *l'esprit anglais* in Dickens and Mr. Chesterton, *l'esprit italien* in D'Annunzio? But always in his poetry there is *l'esprit allemand*. Heine was essentially the German of genius, even though he were a Jew.

As with the supremely great, so with the lesser gifted. A recently published omnibus volume contains a hundred stories written by a hundred different Jewish writers, and if there were such a thing as a common Jewish culture, a common Jewish *point d'appui*, they surely should be apparent in a collection of this sort. A considerable portion of the stories are concerned with Jewish subjects, but they are the work of writers apparently either still living in eastern Europe or still affected vitally by the ghetto atmosphere. The essentially Western writers, even as when as is the case with the late Israel Zangwill and Mr.

Louis Golding, they are concerned with Jewish subjects, as it seems to me, write much more as Englishmen than Jews, and do not suggest any particular
difference in judgment to that possessed by the average Englishman. Benjamin Disraeli is included, and
certainly though he was not a Jew by religion, few
Jews have so successfully retained the flamboyancy
of the Oriental. But except that he was flamboyant,
Disraeli, the writer, was quite definitely English, and
his flamboyancy was no greater than that of many of
his French contemporaries.

Tristan Bernard is included. But what is there
Jewish in his Palais Royal farces? André Maurois is
included, but I can find nothing that is not eminently
and distinctively French in his witty and acutely intelligent judgment. Alfred Sutro is included, and who
more respectably English than he? Leon Feuchtwanger and Arnold Zweig are included, two writers
eminently and entirely Teutonic. Stefan Zweig is included. He is best known in England from his illuminative study of Verhaeren, the Flemish poet. I chal-
lenge any critic to find in that admirable piece of constructive criticism any suggestion of a Jewish point of
view. Similarly, Georg Brandes, the Dane, one of
the greatest of modern literary critics, whose essays
on Shakespeare are of outstanding value, writes always
as a European, which he was, and never as an Asiatic,
which he certainly was not. Marcel Proust, the most
discussed of modern novelists, was a Jew, but I doubt
whether any patriotic or cultured Jew could find anything Hebraic in Proust's art or in his attitude to life.

"Proust is completely detached from all modern moral considerations," said a recent critic; "there is no right and wrong in Proust nor in his world." Perhaps the two most gifted living Jewish writers in England are Siegfried Sassoon, the poet, and Philip Guedalla, and in neither of them, so far as I am able to understand, is there any suggestion of quality derived from their heredity and not from their environment.

For many years the Jew has held high and honourable place in the world of music. But the late Lord Redesdale has recorded that Joachim, that fine austere artist, once deplored the fact that there never had been a Jewish composer of the very first rank.

In his *Judaism in Music,* Wagner says:

> This art of talking without saying anything is one for the cultivation of which music offers exceptional opportunity; for the reason that the great masters have already said in it all that it is capable of expressing as a separate art. This once done, all that followed could be but after-babble, the very correctness of which, so painful and deceptive, reminded one of the way in which parrots are taught to imitate human speech; for it was naturally as bereft of all true expression as the familiar performances of those stupid birds. Yet even in this apish tongue there is a specially Jewish style of utterance, and our Jewish music makers have in it a dialect as special to their race as the one already described.

That is sheer nonsense. The modern Jewish composers may never have been supremely great and original, but they have certainly never written in "a specially Jewish style". What is there Jewish in

Mendelssohn's incidental music to *A Midsummer Night's Dream*? What is there Jewish in Meyerbeer's *Les Huguenots*? Offenbach was a Jew, and he is said to have set the Second French Empire to music. And it is a curious and suggestive example of the Jewish power of assimilation, as I have before remarked, that two of the most successful composers of modern jazz music, which of course derives from negro tunes, are Irving Berlin and George Gershwin, both of them Jews.

The most famous of all Jewish painters is Joseph Israels, the Millet of Holland, who was the son of a Jewish money-lender and was originally intended for a rabbi. Until he was twenty-one, Israels lived in an entirely Jewish circle, and it was not until he went outside that circle, first to study in Paris, and then to live with simple Dutch folks on the Holland coast, that he became a great painter. "He pictured the tragedies of common life which all have experienced and all can understand." It was the common life of Holland, and not of the ghetto that he pictured. Israels was a Dutch, and not a Jewish artist.

"The physical perceptions of the Jews", wrote Wagner, "have never resulted in sending forth from their ranks any plastic artists; their vision having been always too steadily fixed upon things far more practical than beauty and the spiritual contents of a world of imagination. Thus as far as my knowledge extends, we have no record of any Jewish architect or sculptor in our time." This was written in 1850. The reason why there has been no great Jewish achievement in plastic art has certainly nothing to do with lack of imagination or with preoccupation with money-making. The Jewish horror of idolatry induced a disinclination to create any kind of graven image, and this was intensified by the Hebraic reaction against the Hellenic joy in physical beauty.

Since Wagner wrote, Jacob Epstein has arisen to add to the world's great sculptors. Writing of Epstein's art, P. G. Konody says : " He finds in every human face just what he looks for—and he does not look for prettiness or charm. That his portrait busts of women have a beauty of their own is undeniable —the beauty of fierce primitive races in whom the animal instincts are not hidden under the veneer of civilisation." With the power of his tremendous personality Mr. Epstein has produced what is now known as the Epstein type: " a curious perversity seems to make him search among his white models for the high cheek bones and protruding lips and eyes of the dark races." I am not concerned to estimate the value of Epstein as an original artist, a task for which I have no sort of qualification, but Konody's description of his work, which seems to me absolutely accurate, certainly does not suggest that obsession with things of the spirit which is the Hebrew cultural tradition. In his sketches there is a melancholy which has been described as Jewish, but which again I suggest may be much more properly regarded as a heritage from the atmosphere of eastern Europe.

" The Hebrew mind," says Mr. Leon Simon, " looks inward from the start. It does not take man for granted as part of the physical universe, but fastens precisely on that which seems to divide him from the the rest of nature, and is at pains to explain how he comes to be able to distinguish good from evil. Its postulates, the things that it accepts as given, are good and evil, not the sun and the moon and the stars. It has no particular interest in things physical and physical standards of value. Its one abiding reality is a God who is pure spirit, and whose distinguishing characteristic is that he knows good from evil. It is in a sense true that the Hebrew, no less than the Greek, interprets the universe in terms of himself; but he interprets it in terms of his spiritual self. He is not inclined to remake the sun and the sea in his own physical image. His first care is to subordinate the whole of the physical universe to the perfected image of himself as a moral being."

This very interesting passage is open to considerable criticism. It is exact if it is only applied to Hebrew culture as it is expressed in the Prophets, but is surely inexact if it is applied to the superb singer who wrote the Song of Songs, and who, in common with the majority of poets, was compelled " to remake the sun and the sea in his own physical image ".

"How fair and how pleasant art thou, O love, for delights!

" This thy stature is like to a palm tree, and thy breasts to clusters of *grapes*.

" I said, I will go up to the palm tree, I will take hold of the boughs thereof: now also thy breasts shall be as clusters of the vine, and the smell of thy nose like apples ; "

JEWISH CULTURE

It must always be difficult exactly to define the characteristics of any culture. For example, how different a thing is the outlook on life latent in the sermons of Jeremy Taylor, in the sonnets of Shakespeare, and in the novels of Charles Dickens. There is, however, in the art and literature of the European countries a certain vague but not unreal continuity. Thus the spirit of the Prologue to Chaucer's *Canterbury Tales*, of the comedy scenes in Shakespeare and of the Dickens novels, all suggest the same kind of people with the same kind of essential characteristics. It might therefore be expected that, with the Jew's miraculous continuity made possible only by his fidelity, in face of the bitterest persecution, to the traditional religion of his fathers and to the most ancient of all codes of law, there should be discovered in Jewish literature, in whatever language it be written, something of that Hebrew culture which Mr. Simon has described.

I have suggested that there is little or no suggestion of it in Heine or in any of the lesser writers to whom I have referred. It will be at once answered that the Jew, writing in the language of the country in which he lives, is, to an extent, the assimiliated Jew, naturally affected by the artistic and cultural atmosphere in which he is working and that the continuance of the Jewish spirit must be sought in the literature produced in modern times in Hebrew and in Yiddish. There is a surprisingly extensive Yiddish literature written in the Russian Pale, and more recently in America. Among the best known of the modern

Yiddish poets is Maurice Rosenfeld, who emigrated from eastern Europe to America, and who, in
his two books of poems, "Songs of the Ghetto" and
"Songs of Labour", has expressed with plaintive
force the sorrows of the victims of the sweater. One of
Rosenfeld's poems "To the New Year", is included
in a volume of translations by Bertha Beikinstadt,
published in Cape Town. I quote the first and the last
two stanzas:

> Yet another year has passed
> And it leaves us at the last
> In a flood of bitter tears,
> Yet another year is dead,
> Which has filled our souls with dread
> And has tortured us with fears.
>
> . . . . .
>
> Sink, old year, and disappear
> For a fresh young year is here.
> Ah, how innocent and fair
> In his bright and smiling eye,
> Surely he will ne'er belie
> The fair promise glowing there.
>
> He is young and he is kind,
> Sin has not yet stained his mind,
> Naked comes he in the frost.
> Enter in, O New Year fair,
> Though we know not what you bear,
> Hope in thee we have not lost.

Even in translation this is good moving writing, but
its spirit is the spirit of revolt against social conditions,
shared alike by Gentile and Jew, and in it I can find
no sort of trace of any definite Hebraic point of view.

Of the modern Hebrew poets, Chaim Nachman
Bialik is one of the most famous. Mr. Israel Cohen
describes him as "an impassioned votary of the

national idea ''. I have read some of Bialik's poems in
Bertha Beikinstadt's translations, and in two or three
of them there is this national idea expressed in modern
terms. But Bialik is also a poet much concerned with
his own personal emotions who expresses himself in
an imagery that is certainly far more European than
Hebrew. The translations are a little clumsy, and I
daresay do not entirely express the spirit of the
original. I quote the last stanzas of a poem, '' O give
me cover 'neath thy wing '':

> The silver stars beguiled me with their sheen,
>   It was a dream—it too, hath passed and flown;
> And now, naught have I in the wide, wide world—
>   Naught! Now I am alone.
>
> O give me cover 'neath thy wing, be thou
>   A mother unto me, a sister dear,
> Let for my head thy bosom refuge be
>   For my unanswered prayers a sweet nest here.

And I ask again, is this distinctively Jewish? It
must be remembered that the gloom, the apprehension and the despair which characterize, and quite
naturally characterize, Hebrew and Yiddish literature
produced in pre-revolution Russia, or by emigrants
to America, born and bred in a Russian atmosphere,
are also the characteristics of the great pre-revolution
Russian writers from Gogol to Tchekhov. No Yiddish
writer could be more grey than Dostoievsky—Tolstoi,
who disliked him, said that there was '' something
Jewish in his blood ''—or Tchekhov, of whom Gorki
has written: '' Reading Anton Tchekov's stories one
feels oneself in a melancholy day of late autumn, when

the air is transparent and the outline of naked trees, narrow houses, greyish people is sharp. Everything is strange, lonely, motionless, helpless."

The mood of the Jew is the mood of his environment. He reacts to his surroundings. Against all his instincts and all his prejudices, his real spiritual home is his material home. He has made and will doubtless continue to make contributions of outstanding value to the treasures of civilization, to its culture and to its art, but, those contributions are made, not from the outside, but from the inside, not by strangers, but by natives, not by men owing their inspiration to some foreign influences, but from men who ' belong ' and who are to be counted among the fine flowers of the society of which they form a part.

CHAPTER 7

—AND TO-MORROW

THE Jews are the people of the prophets, but he would be a bold man indeed who would prophesy concerning the Jews. All the circumstances set out in the preceding chapters, when taken together, present an overwhelming case for the belief that the Jews must sooner or later disappear as a separate and distinct community. In western Europe, and in America, intermarriage is becoming more and more common. And there is a concensus of opinion that the Westernized Jew becomes, as the generations pass, less and less faithful to the traditional religion, which, above all other things, has preserved his separatism in a society that, for two thousand years, has been nominally Christian, but which, in its turn, is now growing less and less faithful, not only to the Christian dogma, but also to the Christian traditional ethic. This weakening of religious allegiance on both sides must, it would seem, hasten assimiliation, the same causes operating among the well-to-do in France, Great Britain and America as are operating in Russia, among the bulk of the Jewish population, who are inevitably affected by Bolshevist propaganda and by

the Bolshevist policy which, in this respect, follows
the precedent of sixteenth-century statesmanship and
aims at an entirely homogenous population.

The protagonists of Liberal Judaism are eager to
preserve what they regard as the essentials of the
Jewish religion by bringing its formulas and its pre-
sentation into accord with the incidents of modern
life, and thus by preserving religion, preserving separatism, but Liberal Judaism is becoming so like the
vague Christianity affected by the majority of
twentieth-century Protestants, that the difference between Liberal Jew and Christian modernist is extremely difficult to determine.

The Jew is, however, the most stubborn stock in
the history of mankind. He will intermarry with the
peoples among whom he lives, and even though the
Jewish blood in him may be reduced to twenty-five
per cent, or less, not only do certain Jewish characteristics survive, but he is prouder of the twenty-five per
cent than of the rest of his descent, and, despite persecution, misrepresentation, and ridicule, will proudly
acclaim himself the kin of Abraham, Isaac, and of
Jacob. The Jew has never been able to escape from
himself. If he cease to be a Jew, he becomes " an
anomaly, Jew and not Jew in one ".

I have suggested that this intense Jewish feeling
has been stimulated by persecution, and therefore
the assimilation and the consequent disappearance
that seemed almost certain three or four years ago
has now been made improbable by the Nazi persecutions in Germany. The Nazi has proclaimed that the

Jew is the eternal alien in whatever country he lives and to whatever government he owes allegiance.

In an article in the July number of the *Quarterly Review*, Mr. Israel Cohen, acutely aware of the inability of the Jews themselves to do anything more than make provision for a small percentage of the German-Jewish population, urges that the League of Nations should formally protest against the Nazi Jew-baiting. He says that Article 11 of the Covenant of the League justifies such intervention. Mr. Cohen writes:

> There should be no unnecessary delay, therefore, in initiating the action for bringing the matter before the League, so that the Jews in Germany may have restored to them intact the civil, political, and religious rights that they exercised before; and there is no Power that could more appropriately and effectively take such a step, in the interest of justice and humanity, than Great Britain, which cannot be suspected of wishing to exploit the situation for any political reason, which enjoys the repute of traditional protector of oppressed races, and which holds the proud and responsible trust for the establishment of the National Home of the Jewish people.
>
> The handling of this problem will form a crucial test of the power and the utility of the League. Should it prove impossible or impracticable, either on technical or tactical grounds, for the League to effect the deliverance of the Jews in Germany from their tyrannous persecution and to ensure the complete restoration of their former equality, then will the League indeed afford a pitiful demonstration of its impotence. For the League was created, in the spirit of the prophets of ancient Israel, not only to maintain peace between the sovereign nations, but also to secure it for all the peoples of the earth, and there

is no people that needs and deserves it so much as that which has been preaching peace, with unflagging energy and unabated hope, from the time of Isaiah unto the present day. If the League, the guardian of the conscience of mankind, should continue to suffer one of its member States in the heart of Europe to trample upon the rights and liberties of its Jewish denizens and to encompass their destruction by a legalised system of degradation and pauperisation, then its apathy or its passivity would betoken the collapse of the basic principles upon which it was established and the ignominious bankruptcy of modern civilisation.

But Mr. Cohen knows quite well, that whatever may be the paper justification for such action, the League of Nations will not, indeed cannot, interfere in the internal affairs of any of its members, even though the conduct of those internal affairs may ultimately become an international menace. Neither Great Britain nor any other power will do anything to secure for the German Jews the restoration of " the civil, political and religious rights that they exercised before ". The most that can be hoped is that the denunciation of persecution may affect the policy of the German Government and secure some modification of the anti-Jewish ordinances. The impotence of the League may suggest " the bankruptcy of modern civilisation ". I am not inclined to deny that bankruptcy. I think it is likely that the Jew will continue to suffer in the convulsions that may continue for years, incidental to the passing of one era and the beginning of another. Hitlerism is undeniably stimulating anti-Semitism all over the world, and the inevit-

able result must be that the Jew in comfortable
circumstances in England, in France and in America
will be led by the persecution of his fellows to attach
greater value and greater importance to his Jewish
descent, though there is no evidence at present that
Hitlerism will bring into being that Jewish international solidarity which at present only exists in the
imagination of the anti-Semites. But that may come, for
Hitlerism has entirely changed the character of the
Jewish problem, and may have a profound effect on
the future of the Jewish race.

So it seems certain that for many generations
Jewry will continue an indefinite international community, incapable of coherent action, consisting of
men and women who, on the one side, react very
lightly to racial loyalty, while at the other extreme
they hold their Jewish faith and their Jewish descent
as the chief possessions of their lives. Whether they
remain, or whether they are fated in the course of
generations to disappear, no people have put humanity
more greatly in their debt. Their religion has emphasized the essential spirituality of human life. They
have given society in the family the basis of civilization, which has gradually developed, since the beginning of the Christian era, and which is now threatened
by the new sociology and the new morality. They
have emphasized the great fact that here man has no
abiding dwelling-place; that human life is a prelude
to nobler and more satisfying experience; that, in the
words of the Talmud, "life is a passing shadow, the
shadow of a bird in his flight".